IMAGINING
RAMA

IMAGINING RAMA

A brief guide to exploring the universe, mystery and meaning

By James Harlow Brown

First published in 2012 by Lorien Partners Pty Ltd
in partnership with Green Olive Press
PO BOX 145, DARLINGHURST, NSW 1300, AUSTRALIA
www.lorienpartners.com

The Stephen Hawking quote is from A Brief History of Time:
From the Big Bang to Black Holes by Stephen W. Hawking,
published by Bantam Press.
Reprinted by permission of The Random House Group Limited

National Library of Australia Cataloguing-in-Publication entry
Author: Brown, James Harlow.
Title: Imagining Rama: a brief guide to exploring the universe,
mystery and meaning / James Harlow Brown.
ISBN: 9780987330123 (pbk.)
Subjects: Philosophical anthropology.
Spiritual life.
Religion and science.
Dewey Number: 128.4

Publishing services provided by GOPublishing
(www.greenolivepress.com)
Cover illustration: Bhavna Khanna
Cover and internal design: Gloria Tsang/Green Olive Press
Printed in Australia by McPherson's Printing Group

To searchers

There are more things in heaven and earth, Horatio,
than are dreamt of in your philosophy.
—Shakespeare, *Hamlet,* Act 1

AMDG

Contents

Acknowledgements

A number of people have encouraged me and helped me significantly improve this book.

Judy Bamberger and Bram van Oosterhout, my friends in Canberra, for making the book far more "user-friendly." They provided a very large number of suggestions that helped me say much more clearly what I intended to say.

Rev Jorie Manefield Ryan, a friend, poet and priest, who encouraged my approach to the great mystery and who suggested a better way to handle the poetry in the book.

Suzanne Mercier, a friend, for suggesting a number of clarifications that made the book more understandable.

John Brown, my brother, for noticing some unnecessary complexity I had introduced in my overall approach.

Patrick Brown, my son, for reading an early version and making some valuable suggestions.

Nicholas Brown, my grandson, for noticing several mistakes in my treatment of Star Wars.

David Wansbrough, a professor and poet, who made some suggestions about writing style.

Hacy Tobias, my wife and an author herself, who generously put up with my total immersion in polishing the book for many months.

Joe Pilone, a friend in Sydney, Graham Player, a friend in Hong Kong, and Mike Suzuki, a friend in Philadelphia for their review and valuable comments.

I also wish to acknowledge Caroline Webber, my publisher at Green Olive Press, for her early encouragement, which helped me decide to publish Imagining Rama, and Bhavna Khanna for her wonderful illustrations, which add a great deal to the book.

Preface

A friend of mine, after reading the manuscript of this book asked, "Why would a single mom, with three kids, struggling to earn enough money to keep a roof over her family's head, want a guide to explore her place in the universe?" I immediately explained what I thought the value of my book could be to that single mom (if she could ever make time in her packed schedule to read it). "She has one of the most important jobs in the world; raising three human beings to understand who they are and who they can become. My book can remind her of the bigger picture and the importance of what she does day after day."

That is a good summary of what I'm trying to accomplish in this guide. It is only when we understand the larger *context* for life that we begin to understand the importance of what we are doing with our lives. Context was what the stonemason used when answering the question, what are you doing with that chisel? "I'm building a cathedral." I want to help that single mom reaffirm, as she reads my book, that in a way, she is building three "cathedrals" whose lives will have ripple effects on many, many generations of people in the future.

Of course, the importance of context applies to everyone; the father with the stay at home wife, kids, working long hours, hardly ever seeing his family, paying a huge mortgage and wondering what it is all about. The small business owner who works six days a week to keep her head above water, wanting to believe that the work she is doing is of lasting value. It is a case of making time to become aware, learn and reflect in order to place our daily struggle into a larger and more significant context.

A key problem with our exciting modern world is busy-ness—and the challenges it presents to us. I believe we must *make time* to reflect on larger questions like what is the context for my life? What is a human being anyway, and what does it mean to live well? That is why this is a "brief" guide—to allow you to quickly touch on many things, and whet your appetite for more. My objective is not to convince you that my ideas are correct, but to converse with you and stimulate your appetite to understand more.

Rather than telling you exactly what I will cover right up front, I would like you to trust me and follow me on a journey through the pages of this book. I have found from years of practice that most people learn better about such things through experience rather than explanation. In that regard I suppose I'm a bit like Arthur Stace, the homeless man in Sydney, Australia, who wrote the word "Eternity" in chalk on the city sidewalks for over forty years. He wanted people to encounter something that would trigger their imagination and expand their horizons about living. That is my hope as well.

Once, long ago, I had a mysterious encounter, not with Stace's word "eternity", but with an experience that changed my life. One result was that I became aware that I was a passenger on the planet Earth. I began to wonder where the world and I were headed, and why. I developed a strong need to be "standing on granite" in my beliefs about the cosmic trip I was on, which led me on a search lasting almost thirty years and, finally, to write this book.

Other people have told me about similar experiences, of feeling uneasy in their beliefs and their search for certainty. I began to see that to be human was to question, to be in doubt—to be searching constantly. Despite our most sincere efforts, we are unable to satisfy our curiosity about where our life is ultimately headed. I now understand that we will never reach the end of this search; our desire to know is a gift.

The wonderful thing about this gift of curiosity is that it lures us to explore things beyond our usual horizons. We choose our personal horizons by focusing on our everyday roles, activities, interests and concerns. Yet, if we dare to venture beyond our usual limits, a new vantage point may emerge, and reveal opportunities to see ourselves—and the entire universe—from a fresh and expansive perspective. And, if we are able to do that, we may perceive the context of our life and our personal destiny very differently, and begin to live differently. The poet W. B. Yeats sensed this when he wrote:

> The winds that awakened the stars
> Are blowing through my blood.[1]

Of course, there is the opposite opinion. What I have just described as a wonderful possibility is called pure fantasy by some. The American Philosopher Suzanne Langer expressed this position very succinctly, ". . . the pattern of human evolution (like) the tendency of individual growth, in persons as in races, (goes) from dreamlike fantasy to realistic thinking." [2] I will not argue my position is true and Langer's 'realistic thinking' is false. My hope is to awaken a desire in you to journey further into the unknown and decide for yourself. That way, you can begin to see the largest possible context for everything that exists, and the potential importance of your own everyday "ordinary" living.

Chapter 1

RAMA

And your young men shall see visions,
and your old men shall dream dreams.[3]

In 1972, the famous science fiction writer Arthur C. Clarke wrote a novel entitled *Rendezvous with Rama*. In the opening of the story, scientists discover a mysterious object entering our solar system and send a team of astronauts to investigate. When they land, the astronauts find that what they thought was an asteroid is instead a massive hollow cylinder. Suddenly, a door in the end of the cylinder opens to admit them, and the mystery deepens. A strange world is asleep inside.

As the astronauts climb down an eight-kilometer-long staircase to the floor of the cylinder, it begins to awaken and come alive, apparently programmed to respond to a human presence. The remainder of the novel deals with the astronauts' discovery of the intriguing processes of the artificial world that Clarke calls "Rama"—named after a Hindu God, relating to the god-like attributes of the cylinder's unknown makers. At the end of the novel, Rama changes course away from the Earth and exits our solar system. Arthur C. Clarke, in this first of a series of books featuring Rama, does not yet reveal its mysterious purpose.

Imagine that you are one of the astronauts sent to explore Rama. You have just landed on the outer surface of the enormous dark object and stand looking back at the Earth in the distance. Everything familiar is far away on that faint speck of light, and you are surrounded by strangeness. Abruptly, a great entrance door to Rama swings open, and you climb down an immense staircase into the black interior. As you enter, the lights of Rama turn on and it gradually reveals its marvels to you. You are awed at the intricate workmanship of the world built inside a fifty-kilometer-long, sixteen-kilometer-diameter cylinder. A question creeps into your mind: are there inhabitants? For the first time since entering Rama you feel a premonition that something is missing. Your imagination begins to work on the puzzle of Rama's apparent emptiness. Perhaps its original owners left long ago, but you can find no residue or evidence of this. Maybe it was built for someone who never used it, or maybe it has been waiting for its intended users. Who sent Rama into our solar system, and why?

In this book, I will use Rama as a metaphor for our universe. We humans are inside a surprising, self-contained reality much like Rama: a mystery-filled universe that is gradually awakening and changing before our eyes. On the vast scale of the multi-billion year timeline of the universe, we have only recently "opened the door" to our own Rama. Our growing knowledge and tools have increasingly revealed its secrets, enabling us to go "inside" this reality. In the 5,000 short years of humanity's scientific history, we have barely begun our exploration of the universe.

Up until very recently, science's perspective was that the universe was static and unchanging. Only in the last 150 years or so, has science's understanding advanced to the point where we realize that the universe is "awakening"—evolving and becoming. During the last 80 years astrophysicists have deduced that the universe originated in a primordial "Big Bang" event of explosive creation. Still, science's ways of analyzing reality are quite elementary and limited compared to the scope and subtlety of the universe.

To appreciate the limitations in science's capabilities to explain what we experience, consider this simple example. Scientists cannot accurately predict the motion of a flag waving in a breeze, let alone the behavior of the breeze itself, using the most powerful supercomputers. The best that they can manage are inexact models of flags and breezes that portray only a shadow of the real thing. The same limitations apply to all mathematical representations of reality in physics: from the behavior of galaxies and stars in astrophysics to the minutest elements of matter, energy and space-time in quantum physics. We need to appreciate science's limitations in order to seek other ways to understand the mystery of our own Rama.

These limitations were brought home to me shortly after I went to work at NASA in the early 1960s. I was a computer programmer, responsible for calculating the orbits of scientific satellites around the Earth. We used data from a number of tracking stations around the world, and calculated the position of each satellite using the most sophisticated mathematical models available. We never were able to calculate the exact (real) location of a satellite, and had to constantly correct our predictions for them to be useful. Why? Because the mathematical models we used to describe the Earth and gravity and other important features of a satellite's orbit were approximations. In fact, mathematical models, which are at the heart of science's description of reality, are always approximate. *Mathematics can never completely describe the extraordinary complexity of reality.* Mathematical equations are "ideal" concepts and reality is never exactly like this ideal. Later on, I will describe the significant implications of this difference between simplified human concepts *about* reality and what actually *exists* in reality.

While the achievements of science and technology over the last 400 years have dramatically improved human life, this focus has also left mankind with an unfortunate blind spot, which results from the assumptions we make about the process of human knowing. The widespread modern assumption—that scientists and their knowledge have the last word about reality—arose out of the enlightenment and its emphasis on scientific certainty rather than including other forms of wisdom as well. As a consequence, philosophy has taken a back seat to science, and today is no longer seen by many people as being the essential foundation of human wisdom.

This science-centric way of viewing the world has largely replaced the former assumption about a different way that human beings know reality. This former assumption can be briefly summarized as being "beyond science." Let me be clear: mathematics and science *are* wonderful achievements and valid within their sphere. However, I am raising an important question; are we humans able to "see" other dimensions of Rama through other types of knowing?

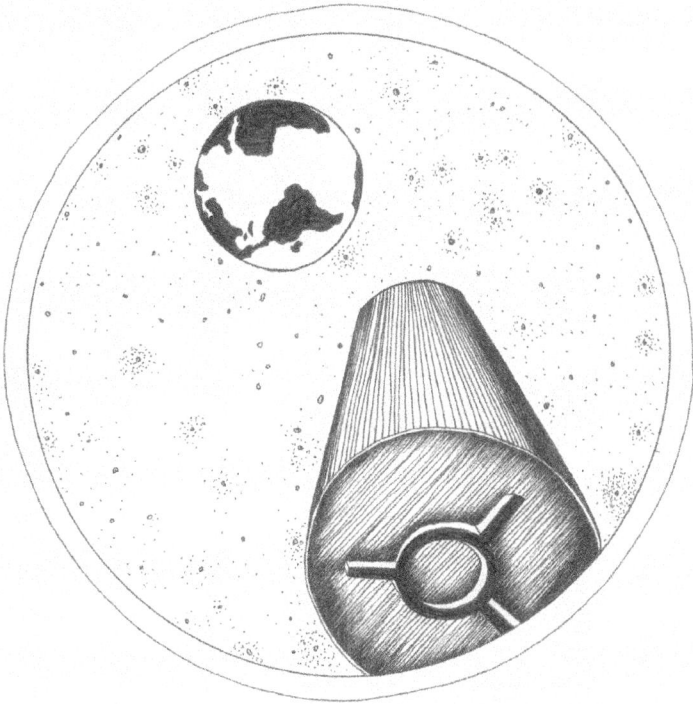

Figure 1—Rama and Earth

Chapter 2

IMAGINATION AND REALITY

We are always ahead of ourselves,
always seeking to bring to fruition
some future goal or idea
—William Macomber [4]

We started our journey with using Rama as a metaphor for the universe—a mysterious reality whose inner workings we humans have barely begun to unlock. Many twenty-first century Westerners struggle to sense the mystery of Rama because our science-centric perspective obscures our view. However, there is a way that we can continue our journey to understand more deeply what Rama really is, and that is by using our imaginations.

Shakespeare summarized our ambivalent feelings about and even suspicion of imagination as a valid source of knowledge, and yet its promise:

> Lovers and madmen have such seething brains,
> Such shaping fantasies that apprehend
> More than cool reason ever comprehends.
> The lunatic, the lover, and the poet
> Are of imagination all compact. [5]

Imagination is simply the mental process of forming concepts and images about things that may or may not be real. Our insights and intuitions are not formed or strictly managed by reason; so imagination remains open to possibilities. Thus, imagination is a good tool to help us see what might lie beyond the limitations of our usual way of seeing Rama.

Poets, writers and other artists treasure the power of imagination. They do not start with logic or reason to create a work of art; they start with their imagination, driven by an urge to create. Carol Joyce Yates, the American writer expressed the experience of artistic imagination like this. "One of the motives for creating art is a feeling of homesickness, that you've lost something. That is very powerful and haunting and you cannot quite get to it in your conscious life. Through your imagination you inhabit this invisible and palpable place." [6] Regardless of how they might express their own experience, every artist would recognize the authenticity of Ms Yates's statement about the power of imagination.

We can imagine almost anything. Still, our imaginings only become believable when they reasonably "fit" with our everyday world and build upon our experiences to achieve new, expanded possibilities. The modern fairy tales of science fiction build on our ordinary experiences of space, time, and consciousness by assuming that they have no limitations, expanding our vision of the mystery of the universe.

One common device science fiction uses to trigger our imaginations is altering our ordinary perspective of time. In the nineteenth century, Jules Verne wrote believably of space travel in the future, giving the scientists of his day a reasonable interval to invent space travel. Similarly, in twenty-first century stories, when our view of time stretches into the distant future, we can imagine, and sense it might actually happen, that humanity will be able to build planets and even create artificial life, ultimately governing the entire universe. The movie *Star Wars* seems plausible to us because of our feeling that the story is far distant in time—"long ago in a galaxy far away"—which allows humanity to possibly achieve its technological marvels. In this instance, imagination hints to us that our everyday concepts about mankind's potential may be far too ordinary.

We can also imagine time from another perspective, one in which the past, present, and future have no boundaries between them. In the movie *Back to the Future,* a young man travels back in time and visits his parents in the 1950s while they are still in high school, before they married and he was born. The young man rescues his future father from being hit by a car and discovers, to his horror, that it was this particular accident that originally led to his parents meeting and subsequently marrying. He had unwittingly prevented his own birth by altering the past! He saves the day by encouraging his future father to stand up to the school bully—something his father never would have done in the original past—by re-inventing events so that his future mother is attracted by his father's courage, and not out of pity as before. This small act by the young man has far-reaching consequences into the future—the1980s—transforming his entire family for the good, simply due to a difference in the starting point of his parents' marriage, based on mutual respect rather than dependency. Many in the movie audience, witnessing this imaginative perspective of time, sensed the hidden power of small acts to ripple into the future in ever-widening interactions.

Science fiction also expands our perspectives of space and consciousness. The variations are limitless because anything might be possible in the distant, unknown reaches of the universe. The most interesting stories in this vein portray the encounters between humans and alien beings. In *E.T.,* perhaps like no other movie, the hope of connection with and even the possibility of love between humans and aliens are captured. The reward for the boy who befriends E.T. is shown symbolically—the touch of E.T.'s glowing fingertip leaves the boy with some unknown yet magical legacy. The audience is certain that the boy (and they) have been touched by love. Most of us want to believe that the universe *is* friendly to mankind. Imagination makes us aware of this desire, while rational thought largely ignores it.

As these science fiction movies illustrate, imagination can make us aware of things that reason may miss. Imagination suggests that reality is a subject that demands reflection. Are our everyday experiences any more "real" than those which science fiction imagines in a future time, on a distant star, within a friendly universe? Many people would say, and believe absolutely, that the only "reality" is here and now, in things they can see, touch, taste, and feel. Yet, at the same time, many of these same people respond with questions or joy or amusement or awe when their imaginations are stimulated by the possibilities presented through science fiction. These instinctive human responses hint to us about the hidden mysteries of reality.

It is important to look more closely at how our minds use imagination. The scientific way of knowing views everything as objects then simplifies these objects into concepts and mathematical models so that its logic can deal with them. But the human mind can know things in another way involving what the theologian Karl Rahner calls "original knowing". Rahner sees mankind as having two types of knowing originating from different sources in the mind. At the rational, scientific source, the object we want to know is perceived as something outside the mind, presented as a limited object or concept. The other source of knowing in our mind, "original knowing," is our knowing of ourselves and our union with reality. Rahner sees all human knowledge originating from both these sources. "In knowledge not only is something known, but the subject's knowing is always co-known." [7]

Original knowing is difficult to understand and impossible to define precisely, which makes us uncomfortable. When we try to grasp it we cannot. It is as if this source of knowing is behind us, and when we turn around to try to see it, it is still behind us. We can never unravel how we do this kind of original knowing. There are no rules for it, no logic that we can use to control it. When we focus our attention on original knowing and try to bring it to the rational source of objective knowing to analyze it, it flees from us. It is this mysterious source of original knowing in our minds that gives imagination its scope and power to first sense then know what is beyond science. The French Philosopher Jacques Maritain referred to this original knowing as "the preconscious life of the intellect". [8] Human knowing, especially poetic intuition, emerges from a deep source below our consciousness which somehow links us with "what is". It gives every human being the capacity to know reality more broadly than science.

Rahner's and Maritain's concepts of knowing go beyond science's objectivity, leave reality whole, and give humanity a capacity to know that which is mysterious. This power to know constantly breaks through into our awareness—whether we allow ourselves to sense it or not—as creative imagination or intuition; for example, as the hints of questions or joy or awe that science fiction stories reveal. I will use creative imagination in this book to help you to better sense this awesome power in yourself.

In the next two chapters, I will examine three basic concepts: time, space, and consciousness. By looking at these in imaginative ways, I hope to help you sense the mystery in Rama.

Chapter 3

TIME

What then is time?
If no one asks me, I know.
If I want to explain it to a
questioner, I do not know.
—Augustine.[9]

W hy do I start an exploration of the universe with the concept of time? For two reasons. It is easy to take time for granted in everyday life. I want to help you discover that things (like time) that appear ordinary may be extraordinary. Second, time plays a much larger role in the universe than most people imagine. This chapter lays the groundwork for seeing, in the chapters that follow, that time is one of the most important *creative* forces in our own Rama.

To a physicist, time is not simple. In fact, in the last hundred years a great deal of study has gone into understanding the role time plays in shaping the universe. As the origins of the universe have become clearer—the universe as we know it came into existence more than 13,000,000,000 years ago in a "Big Bang"—scientists realized that time also originated in that event. They also discovered that time does not necessarily flow just from the past through the present to the future. Rather than being the commonplace, clock-bound quantity we are all familiar with, physicists discovered problems to be solved about time.

Our everyday experience of time is such an intimate part of our language and life that it is difficult to imagine it any differently. We are confident that events happen either in the past, present or future. Time is evenly spaced; clocks divide it into seconds and hours, and calendars, into days and years. What could be more obviously true? It seems that time has been the same straightforward quantity throughout mankind's history. For thousands of years, time has passed in regular intervals. It seems as unchangeable and as reliable as clocks are accurate. And, as a starting point it is reasonable to say that our ordinary experiences of time are probably valid. But there are also unusual things about time.

Our sense of time is a product of our consciousness, and as such can be changed by our circumstances. The more information we remember about a particular experience, the longer the remembered duration of the experience seems to us. Happy experiences seem to be more organized in our brains, take up less information storage room, and thus seem to be of shorter duration in our consciousness. After all, time flies when you're having fun. Einstein once jokingly explained. "When you sit with a nice girl for two hours, it seems like two minutes; when you sit on a hot stove for two minutes, it seems like two hours. That's relativity." [10]

Time is not a stand-alone entity. It is deeply connected to both space and consciousness as Einstein's Special Theory of Relativity points out. It is involved in creating the reality of space and consciousness. Space and consciousness have a past, present and future—which says that they are changing, with time's involvement. Einstein perceived time as a fourth dimension of space. As velocities approach the speed of light, both time and space shrink when measured by an observer moving at that speed, compared to an observer who is not moving. Experimental evidence from both astronomy and nuclear physics supports this theory.

Both the previous ideas call into question our certainty concerning the duration of time—it is not as simple a matter as it first seems. There is something else that is unusual about time, from an historical point of view. Rather than time being experienced today in the same way as it was thousands of years ago, there is evidence that mankind's perceptions of time have evolved over the centuries. We are experiencing an "upheaval in our lifetime," as Alvin Toffler observed in his book *Future Shock.*[11] According to Toffler, we are experiencing far more change in our lifetimes than did our ancestors— life seems to be speeding up, and the future appears to be rushing toward us compared to our ancestors. Modern mankind has lost the sense that life proceeds at a regular pace, year in, year out. From an historical perspective, mankind's experience and memory of time does not seem to be constant and unchanging.

So, instead of time being the ordinary experience that we take for granted, there is also something beyond the ordinary about time. This "beyond-ness" in ordinary things like time is what we are reaching for in our journey of imagination—hints of the yet-to-be-discovered secrets and even the never-to-be-understood mystery in Rama.

The Bohemian poet Ranier Maria Rilke sensed the mystery in time in his Ninth Duino Elegy. Seen in this poetic sense, time somehow seems linked to a deep, almost indescribable feeling of strangeness that we experience at certain moments. Even though Rilke does not mention time explicitly, using words like "fleeting" and "once and only once" to suggest its presence, we sense that it is a vital force in creating our lives.

> Because this fleeting sphere
> appears to need us—
> in some strange way
> concerns us: we . . .
> most fleeting of all.
> Once and once only for
> each thing—then no more.
> For us as well. Once.
> Then no more . . . ever. [12]

As we try to analyze Rilke's poetic intuitions about time, they flee from our mind's grasp. Yet, they emerge when we do not grasp for them. Such experiences can enrich our knowledge about reality if we trust them. So how can we "not-grasp" for time in order to imagine it and experience it in a fresh way?

To me, the easiest approach involves dealing with a different dimension of time than that which we normally experience directly: the dimension of human perspective. Perspective depends on the self-awareness of the observer, and his or her location with respect to that which is being observed. In spatial terms, it is easy for us to visualize the dimension of perspective—you "stand back" from something to put it "in better perspective." You remove yourself in space from the thing you want to see in a broader or different way, instead of its normal orientation or detail. But how do we remove ourselves from the usual detail of time that surrounds us to get a perspective of time? This is a difficult question because there is no place we can go to be away from time. In a way, we are asking how we can tap into Rahner's source of original knowledge to let the entirety of time emerge imaginatively.

What follows is my own personal intuition of such an expansive perspective of time. This is intended only as a demonstration and not as the truth about time. I strongly encourage you to create your own imaginative ideas about time to add to or replace mine.

I imagine time is like an event such as a concert. The concert's richness comes from all the preparation that preceded the event in the past—the band's rehearsals, the members' decisions to become musicians, indeed the entire history of mankind's use of sounds to entertain or evoke meaning. Another source of the concert's richness is the uniqueness of the present evening's event, even if the band has played these songs or symphonies hundreds of times. As any performer will tell you, the audience influences the performance. Finally, there is the mysterious influence that the future has on the event. If you think of what an architect did in shaping a building like the Sydney Opera House, bringing his sense of future possibilities into present reality, you will get the idea. The Danish Architect Jørn Utzon saw a vision of the sail-like shape of the building's roof complementing the sailing boats in the harbor, which he used to create an image of great beauty. This vision of beautiful possibility of what the music means, which the composer, the conductor, and each member of the orchestra and audience has, is what reaches into the event and shapes it. Time is like an event in its richness. Every human being, in this sense, is a unique event, participating in creating the richness of time freely, yet influenced by every other event.

Time is also an event that is continuously growing: countless events of time unfold like a flower blooming. This blooming of time's events wraps all the influences of the entire universe into a unique growing flower. The most distant star's light arrives to perfect its color and texture each moment it unfolds. All the events of human consciousness enrich the growing time event. Each person's event of time is a unique petal of the unfolding bloom, and humanity's co-mingled history, poetry, love, and knowledge add charm to its exquisite fragrance. The growing flower of time seems to stretch back, almost forever. Within this incredible flower of time, everything is related to everything else in all directions.

Yet the flower's unfolding process is even more intricate. New flowers burst unexpectedly from within older ones. The flower's shape seems to unfold at an orderly pace for a while, then changes radically to a new shape and assumes an accelerated pace of unfolding. From my imagined perspective, I can name the flower's shapes as I choose—chaos then order then freedom then accelerating newness, and perhaps more chaos before ultimate order. Ordinary days, years, and centuries are contained in each of these shapes, but also the acceleration sensed by Toffler. The dynamism and sweep of the imaginative blooming flower of time overwhelms our ordinary perceptions. The flower's explosion of dynamic unfolding events is time actively participating in the all-consuming process of universal becoming. Such is time in my imagination, as mystery reaches out to me as I reflect. The only word I can conceive to describe it is *beautiful.*

As I said, I do not claim truth for the flower of time, although, to me, it fits many of my experiences, intuitions, and hopes. It is obvious that our everyday concept of time is far more useful for keeping appointments or doing science. It is not practical in daily life to leave ordinary things like time so open-ended. So, why deal with this imaginative perspective as if it had some significance for the here and now?

It seems necessary to me to view ordinary things from such an imaginative perspective on occasion; else we may lose the profound respect due to them. We have, as the German Philosopher Heidegger pointed out, made ordinary things too ordinary in our time by robbing them of their possible transcendence (beyond-ness). And, more importantly, what is beyond our everyday experience may have some deep significance for us, which we ought not ignore.

There is also urgency in seeking such an imaginative perspective. The possibility of mystery lurks everywhere in Rama, and we dare not miss it. As Zen Buddhism teaches, "When logic dies, the secret grows through the eye." Everyone trusts the five physical senses, as well as our ability to reason, but few of us trust our imagination. We sometimes follow our intuitions but seldom wonder where they come from.

It seems to me, however, that the very fact that we are intrigued by the possibility of mystery in ordinary things like time suggests that perhaps we should trust these hints of mystery more. Maybe that which is beyond (or inside) our ordinary existence is trying to attract our attention using the only tool at hand: wonder. But to be more open to these hints, and to learn to trust them, we must first admit to ourselves that our usual perceptions are limited by our everyday ideas about Rama. Our only choice to reach beyond our ordinary perceptions of the universe is to place some trust in our intuitive sense. Otherwise our vision of Rama and the context for our life will always be limited. To me, this is the urgent purpose in exploring these imaginative perspectives—to free us from our potential blind spot and allow us to begin to see Rama as it really may be.

Figure 2—The Events and Blooming of Time

Chapter 4

SPACE AND CONSCIOUSNESS

Poets are in the vanguard of
a changed conception of Being.[13]
—Martin Heidegger

I encouraged you to imagine time as not simply being a straight line from the Big Bang to the distant future but as something organic and growing, with each event in Rama being influenced by every other event. The next step in imagining Rama is to look below the surface of two other aspects of everyday reality from which we can never escape—the cosmic "containers" of space and consciousness.

A starting point for the ordinary reality of space and physical existence is that the human mind really does see something "out there"—space and its contents. While some thinkers have questioned whether reality actually exists outside of our minds, most agree that we live in surroundings that are real. However, things are not so clear when it comes to stating a common viewpoint about consciousness.

A commonplace idea about consciousness is Descartes's, "I think, therefore I am." The "I" is an obvious unit of human consciousness. Everyone would agree that their "I" exists. But what of consciousness beyond the "I"? Based on their ordinary experiences, most humans would agree that "You" exists in the form of numerous other humans. So, a basic idea about consciousness is that the universe contains separate "units" of consciousness that we call "I" and "You"; and that in addition, this thing we call "consciousness" is not subject to the same kind of physical measurement that we can apply to the rest of the universe. Most people would agree with this basic statement. So, what are some of the unusual observations about space and consciousness?

One major question concerning physical existence has arisen in the last 100 years. Prior to the establishment of quantum physics, people believed absolutely that matter consisted of solid lumps of substance created out of basic building blocks of the simplest materials. Quantum physics introduced a contradiction into this seemingly obvious human observation. Physicists found that the basic building blocks of reality are both physical particles and pure energy without substance. Furthermore, it is impossible for mankind to measure precisely how things act at the deeper levels of reality. (The Heisenberg Uncertainty Principle.) Since the 1980s, space and gravity have begun to be described in these same quantum terms. Physicists now speculate that every point in space can be described by ten dimensions, of which humans appear to experience only four: three spatial dimensions and time.[14] At the deepest level of physical existence, including our own bodies, there is a fundamental uncertainty about how we describe matter, and even space-time!

Consciousness, unlike space-time cannot be described mathematically. So, the description of some of the unusual properties of consciousness is necessarily qualitative and based on opinions not scientifically verifiable experiments. The uncommon thing in consciousness that I want to focus on has to do with the word "unit" that I used to limit consciousness. We are individual conscious beings in one apparent way:

we have bodies with limited physical extent. But, is our consciousness isolated within our physical bodies? Does our personal consciousness ever mingle with other consciousnesses?

We could explore the world of psychic phenomena, which in my opinion is heavily populated with self-deluding or fraudulent reporters. It seems more persuasive, therefore, to rely on the evidence of scientists who report on their observations about consciousness with a certain detachment. Perhaps the most respected of these is Abraham Maslow, the noted psychologist.

Maslow studied consciousness extensively throughout his life, and came to the conclusion that it has unusual qualities. In *Toward a Psychology of Being,* he speaks of "the mystery of communication between alone-nesses ("units" of consciousness) via intuition and empathy, love and altruism, identification with others. We take these for granted. It would be better if we regarded them as miracles to be explained." [15] Maslow also described peak experiences—times when humans sense a bond with that which is beyond them. Maslow interviewed people who did not sense that the world is inhabited by units of consciousness confined in aloneness. To the contrary, Maslow found in his research that some people sensed a unity with the universe, and felt integrated with surrounding reality in a way barely describable in words. These anecdotes raise questions about our usual assumption about the separation of matter and consciousness.

The separation or duality of matter and consciousness is one of the most significant assumptions built into the sciences. Scientists assume that space and its contents obey laws and have no mind of their own to alter their ways of acting and interacting. This assumption does not apply to the study of human behavior, but few, if any, scientists believe that atoms, rocks or planets have consciousness.[16] Like our time-sense, this duality assumption is so deeply woven into our thought processes today that we have great difficulty even imagining that it may be only a human device to simplify reality so that our minds can cope with it.

How can we look for hints of the possibility of holistic reality? Part of our problem in gaining a fresh perspective of what we observe in Rama is sensory overload. Mankind never experiences a condition of non-matter and non-consciousness. Yet we must find a way to quiet this overwhelming sensory input if we are to use our imaginations to transcend the insistent ordinary reality of Rama. The *Tao Te Ching* states:

> Numerous colors make man sightless.
> Numerous sounds make man unable to hear.
> Numerous tastes make man tasteless.

To leave our everyday world of the five senses we must use abstraction or pure concepts. Imagine that you are penetrating deeper and deeper into matter and consciousness. You become smaller and smaller—indeed vanishing—in order to reach this level of reality. You cannot see at this deepest level—sight depends on photons, and you are far smaller than light itself, or any of the elementary particles of nature. Nor do any of your senses work for similar reasons. Only your intellect can become small enough to reach this level, in the same way that it can become big enough to encompass the entire universe. What do you encounter at the deepest level of space and consciousness?

When I take this journey, I sense a silent yet pervasive presence, which I will call "being". There is only one being, and everything in the universe that exists above this deepest level shares the same being. Being is neither matter nor consciousness; it just is. Therefore, matter and consciousness, if they are distinct, must differentiate themselves at some higher level of existence. So, is the dualism of matter and consciousness real? Has being, in the reality of the universe we experience, separated into two distinct substances—matter and consciousness? And what about space itself?

Concepts like space are largely metaphorical. For instance, we say "The sun rises and sets." This reflects our human-centered view of the universe. The sun does not really rise or set—the Earth turns and hides the sun as it "sets" and turns some more as it "rises." We use metaphors to view and communicate about almost everything in our Rama.

The word "space" is a metaphor, suggesting emptiness or something missing. If reality were a coffee cup, space would be the empty place where coffee is poured. "Space" is how we commonly experience and refer to the region that surrounds us and the Earth. If we want to imagine the reality of space differently, we need to find another metaphor that avoids the automatic implications of the metaphor "space."

There is a hint of a different metaphor for space in the recent mathematical discovery that ten dimensions are required to describe the geometry of space. These dimensions exist at every point in space so, in this perspective, space is not empty. It is filled with something that physicists describe mathematically, much of which has never yet been observed. These mathematical dimensions are a pure abstraction, without any physical or even metaphorical meaning, at least at present.

What if we imagine that these dimensions—which exist everywhere and completely fill the universe— are the "media" through which being extends itself and acts everywhere? This metaphor brings to mind the various types of materials (media) that artists use to express their inspiration. Composers use sound, which has dimensions of tonality, pitch, etc. Artists use color, which has dimensions of shade, brightness, etc. Poets use words, which have dimensions of sound, meaning, etc. What if we imagine that some cosmic "artist" uses the media we call "space" to create reality from being? The ten dimensions of geometric space are, in this imaginative perspective, an indication of the potential creativity of the artist. Up to now, at least as far as we humans can presently observe, only four of these dimensions have been used by the artist—the three spatial dimensions that are the extent of our universe, and time, which is the creative flow of events of the universe's becoming.

In this strange almost unimaginable world of cosmic artistry that I imagine I can see no reason why matter and consciousness must be distinct. I can, if I wish, imagine that rocks have some consciousness, but less consciousness than plants, and plants far less than humans. Is consciousness shared among all objects? My imagination finds no reason to prevent a degree of sharing of consciousness among all the entities in the universe.

The media of space has almost infinite potential, and our existing world may be only one of many possible artistic works in progress. But how is this media shaped into *our* reality by the cosmic artist? Here we recall Clarke's astronauts and the questions they could not answer. How and why our universe is being created from being is a question that may be beyond our reach, with answers beyond even our imagination.

Stephen Hawking, the noted English Physicist summarized the limits of human answers in *A Brief History of Time*:

What is it that breathes fire into the equations
and makes a universe for them to describe?
The usual approach of science of constructing a
mathematical model cannot answer the questions
of why there should be a universe for the model
to describe. Why does the universe go to all the
bother of existing? [17]

This imaginative perspective is a personal one. The three ideas I have described thus far—time's blooming, being's creativity and the artistic media of "space"—fit with my reflections on my life experiences, and with the wisdom I have studied. This fit is a source of wonder to me. How can the conscious individual that I am imagine such awe-inspiring perspectives? There is a subtle promise in this capacity, and an invitation.

The poet William Blake sensed this mysterious human capacity when he wrote these memorable lines:

To see a World in a Grain of Sand
And a Heaven in a Wild Flower,
Hold Infinity in the palm of your hand
And Eternity in an hour.[18]

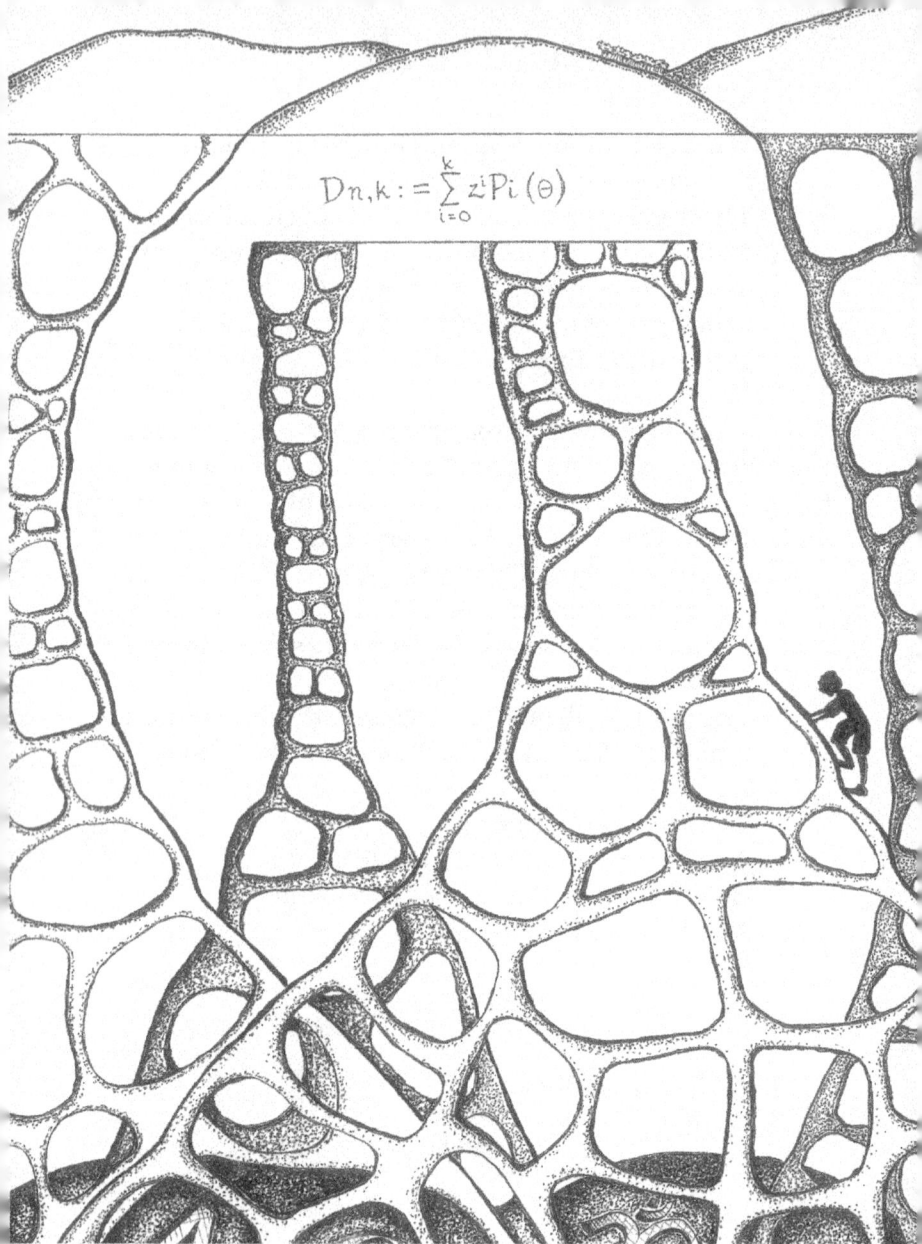

$$D_{n,k} := \sum_{i=0}^{k} z^i P_i(\theta)$$

Figure 3—Being, Space and Consciousness

Chapter 5

FREEDOM

At-homeness in the universe is the fundamental
concern of the human pilgrimage.[19]
—William Schmidt

The artist's media in which each of us lives—space, time, consciousness and other dimensions—is not static but continually changing. We know this but never fully understand it. In this chapter I encourage you to wonder about the mysterious cosmic dynamism in which, perhaps, we play a role.

In Arthur C. Clarke's story, Rama appeared lifeless until the astronauts entered and its dark interior lit up, as if welcoming them. We humans, like Clarke's astronauts have only just "landed" on our own Rama.[20] Like them, we have many questions. Where does our Rama come from? What did its makers intend? Does it have a predetermined purpose? Or is it just a natural thing that exists, with no beginning and no maker? And to include ourselves in these questions as well, how much freedom do we have to change our Rama's direction?

The astronauts had some freedom inside Rama. They could explore it, experiment with its mechanisms and speculate about its makers. But when it came to changing the fictional Rama's path, they were powerless. At a particular point of time, chosen by Rama's builders, the giant cylinder changed course and left the solar system.

At the end of Clarke's trilogy about Rama he explains the purpose of Rama's builders, but in this first book we are left in mystery. Think of Clarke's ability in the Rama trilogy to explain the origin of a single artificial world, and then imagine the immense mystery of our own universe's origin and evolution. Is it possible that we humans can understand its origin or purpose, or can alter its course?

In some science fiction stories superior beings watch the men and women they have created play a "game", trying to follow rules these beings have built into the universe. Mankind's freedom, and the universe's too in this imaginative perspective, is limited. Everything is only free to the degree that the superior beings allow within the rules of the game plan. Ultimately, the payoff of the game for mankind is to perform well on the superior beings' unknown but predetermined judgment scale.

Primitive mankind thought of the "gods" as playing with them, and consequently, primitive religion is largely ritual-based to appease the gods on their own unknown terms. My sense is that twenty-first century mankind retains more than a little of this same belief. It is a major source of a common feeling many people have of being helpless in the face of "forces" bigger than ourselves.

I will explore the cosmos's freedom (including mankind's) by using the term "game plan" as a metaphor. Let me briefly explain this metaphor so you can understand how it is connected to freedom. If you take a game such as football or cricket, the coach has a plan for the game. What are the skills of her players? Which weaknesses in the opponent's players should be exploited? Which of her team's players ought to be in the lineup? While the game is actually being played, during the rapidly changing situations the players face on the field, they freely make decisions of what actions to take, but within the context of the coach's game plan. Of course, they can ignore the coach but she has some authority—but not complete control over them as they play the game—to guide them according to her game plan. She can, for example, call a timeout to remind them about the plan or change plays or players. Winning the game depends on both the insights of the coach and her skill in designing a game plan and the freely given energy and skills of the players in playing the game on the field. I will use this "game plan" metaphor in what follows. I will deal with both the freedom of the cosmos and the mystery of human freedom within the cosmos. Let me start with human freedom.

An extraordinarily wide range of human behaviors, ranging from love and self-forgetfulness to extreme violence and hate is probably the strongest evidence demonstrating seemingly unlimited human freedom. Throughout human history, continuing everyday on television news we see countless examples of self-inflicted pain and terror, self-sacrifice and concern for the innocent. It seems obvious that mankind has radical freedom to act in any manner, unconstrained by predetermined limits on our freedom. In a broader sense, the cosmos itself does not appear to be determined or constrained to take a path of supporting continued existence versus one of destruction. Random catastrophes and the collapse of stars into Black Holes are evidence of this. The universe seems completely free.

What does this apparent absolute freedom imply about an underlying "game plan" for the universe? There are only two possibilities. Either there is no game plan— no rules, constraints, goals, etc., planned into the cosmos or humans in any way—or the game plan, with its rules, goals, etc., is so subtle and non-human that it permits mankind and the cosmos to have almost total freedom. I will imagine that the universe has a game plan and leave it to others to describe a universe without one.[21]

Immediately when we try to imagine a cosmic game plan that also governs mankind, we are confronted with horrific historical facts, which must be explained. How can the Rwanda genocide or a Tsunami killing millions of innocent people be within the rules of a "good" game plan? Some would say that Rwanda and similar atrocities are proof that good is simply a human concept and does not, in fact, exist. Without arguing that point, to me the most persuasive idea about the game plan of the cosmos and mankind is that freedom is rampant, and that the goals and limits that constrain existence, even at their most powerful, are extremely subtle.

What are some hints about the existence of cosmic limits and even goals? One indication of limits within the universe is mankind's intuitive sense of laws that order the cosmos. For example, physicists have discovered the Law of Gravity, which is the universal law of how material attracts other material. There are a number of other laws that scientists have deduced over the centuries that constrain what happens in the cosmos: the absolute speed of light, the laws of Thermodynamics, and others. The Nobel Prize-winning physicist Richard Feynman remarked, "That it is possible to find a rule, like the inverse square law of gravitation, is some sort of miracle." [22] Mankind's insights into such laws is a hint that his intuitive and poetic mind—his imagination— senses some order and possibly even a direction and goals for changes in the universe.

Humanity also senses that there are laws that are appropriate for mankind to follow. At the heart of many of these laws is the fundamental poetic insight that concern for others, and not absolute individual freedom, seems to best fit with some human imperative. Many of humanity's greatest heroes celebrate the triumph of concern for others. Florence Nightingale, Louis Pasteur,

Mother Theresa, Buddha, Jesus—all chose serving others over absolute freedom of self.

But, in practice, we often do not adhere to these implicit laws. Every person knows that other forces come into play when we make choices about how to act on the "playing field." We are said to be controlled, to a significant extent, by our genes, our upbringing, our id, advertising, and numerous other agents. Saint Paul probably put it best over 1,900 years ago when he stated, "I do not understand what I do. For what I want to do I do not do, but what I hate I do." [23]

Mankind's actions in the universe are a bizarre blend of brutality, incredible self-sacrifice, apathy, growth—and every other possible human act imaginable. Although the universe may seem increasingly predictable to physicists, mankind seems unpredictable, without limits, and ever changing. In summary, the cosmos in general and humanity in particular are a puzzle to mankind. To restate the basic question: are the universe and humanity *completely* free or are we being shaped by some game plan?

In the imaginative metaphor I suggest, the "game plan" of the universe relates to both the "players" (humanity) and the "playing field" (the universe we are part of). And, in my metaphor, with a game plan, there must be a "coach"—some entity which has defined a subtle plan for "playing the game" of existence.

I imagine that being, which underlies everything, is involved in the game plan of universal becoming. Like the imaginative concept in Chapter 4, being's role in becoming can best be reached through the realm of abstraction. I imagine the cosmic game plan is called *untamed becoming in universal mutuality*. (By mutuality I mean an exchange between two or more persons, groups or even systems to meet the needs of all.) I will develop this imaginative game plan in two steps, beginning with *untamed becoming,* followed by *universal mutuality.*

Untamed becoming

There is an almost overwhelming richness in everyday life that confronts us when we are open to it. Our life, indeed the entire world is complex, not simple. Yes, the sun rises and sets daily, and our days seem filled with regular tasks at first glance—eating, working, exercising, sleeping, etc. But think for a moment. What is routine or predictable in our own thoughts, behaviors and emotions and those of others? How orderly can we say our life has been up to now, as we look back on it? And, going a bit further afield, what about the global events we see daily on the television? Does life on our planet in the twenty-first century seem constrained and predictable? And to extend this line of thinking even further, in the imaginative perspective for the universe that we imagined in the previous chapters, are the galaxies—billions of them, each with untold billions of stars—only routinely behaving according to humanly understood laws?

Scientists attempt to "tame" the universe with theories about underlying laws. Physicists, Geneticists, and Behavioral Psychologists capture aspects of reality in mathematical laws. Some scientists dream that future research will completely describe everything. Physicists, for example, diligently search for the "GOD" particle, which will unify all the components of space-time's ten dimensions, and a "Grand Theory of Everything", which would allow them to predict where the universe is going.[24] The physicist Brian Greene has written about this in his book *The Fabric of the Cosmos.*

"Maybe the universe has already drawn out the microscopic fibers of the fabric of the cosmos and unfurled them clear across the sky, and all we need to do is learn how to recognize the pattern." [25]

Yet, in the same book, Greene wrote of his awareness that science falls far short of understanding the *really* real:

"Physicists such as myself are acutely aware that the reality we observe—matter evolving on the stage of space and time—may have little to do with the reality, if any, that's out there." [26]

The same poetic sense that Greene speaks of, that, ultimately, we may not be able to completely grasp reality or what drives it to change was shared by the Welsh Poet Dylan Thomas. He was seized by the power of "untamed becoming" when he wrote:

The force that through the green fuse drives
the flower
Drives my green age; that blasts the roots of trees
Is my destroyer.
And I am dumb to tell the crooked rose
My youth is bent by the same wintry fever.[27]

I imagine that, far below the surface of everyday appearances, in a reality sensed by poets, is located this possibility of "untamed becoming". We encountered this in the time synthesis in Chapter 3, in the uncontrolled blooming of time. In Chapter 4, we also imagined the artistic "media" of space-time and consciousness, yet could not penetrate the mystery of how our reality is being created out of being itself. I imagine, therefore, that the deepest level of the cosmos—being itself—is changing in an untamed manner according to some unfathomable game plan. *Nothing in the cosmos is predetermined; all possibilities are open in the future.*

We can sense this openness to all possibilities, for ultimate order or ultimate chaos, in our personal lives. Can we "tame" these possibilities and live as we desire, according to our own consciously chosen game plan? It is too simple to say yes, and assume that every human being can blithely choose success or failure. Life is complex. Human freedom is also too complex to say that anyone can "tame" it and become exactly what they desire. Deep inside ourselves, we know that becoming who we want to be is the work of a lifetime, spent "taming" an unruly inner self. All of these—my own life experiences, the world's unpredictability, and the universe's dynamism—are why I imagine that the first part of the game plan of the cosmos is "untamed becoming." Yet, somehow, I also sense that is not the complete game plan. There's another facet, which I imagine as an invitation to me and every person to play a role in shaping the cosmos's becoming.

Universal mutuality

I imagine that poised against this untamed becoming is the taming activity of universal interdependence. Everything affects everything, even among all the 7,000,000,000 human beings on our planet. "No man is an island," according to poet John Donne. Down through the ages, wise women and men have sensed this universal interdependence and the related power of human mutuality. Today we are beginning to see it ever more clearly, in our growing recognition of the importance of smaller communities as we become more urbanized, and in our increasing awareness, accelerated by the Internet that we live in a "global village." You can also see the desire for universal mutuality in many of the world's religions. The bodhisattvas in Buddhism, rather than retiring from the world, sacrificed their own happiness for the sake of the people.[28] Rabbi Hillel said, "What is hateful to yourself, do not to your fellow man." [29] And Jesus taught, "Do to others as you would have them do to you." [30] A good example of mutuality in modern times is the emergence of nonviolent revolution. Gandhi used mutuality as a core principle—*Satyagraha:* eliminate antagonisms without harming the antagonists themselves.

In my imagination, I see the emergence of universal mutuality in history being accelerated by humanity becoming aware of its desire for community ("we-ness") and interdependence. This is connected to our realization of our emerging role in shaping our planet. The insights of science fiction see the influence of humanity ultimately spreading across the stars. Our intuition of this incredible role for ourselves in the cosmic game plan fills us with wonder.

Teilhard de Chardin, the Jesuit paleontologist who imagined such an ultimate becoming of mutuality, expressed his exultation in his "Hymn to Matter":

> Blessed be you, mighty matter, irresistible march
> of evolution, reality ever new born; you who,
> by constantly shattering our mental categories,
> force us to go ever further and further in pursuit
> of truth.[31]

Alfred North Whitehead, the English mathematician and philosopher, saw this universal becoming of mutuality in terms of beauty—the inherent beauty of our entire cosmos realizing and guiding its own becoming in a process of creative conflict through freely given constraint. Winnie and Ted Brock summarized John Haught's analysis of Whitehead's thought:

The cosmos is an aesthetic reality. . . As the creative advance of the universe brings more and more novelty into the picture, the events of the past are continually given a new and unanticipated significance. As the sea of events that make up the cosmos broadens and deepens, the meaning of each individual happening is itself intensified and widened. Its final meaning, therefore, cannot be determined from its own limited perspective any more than we can determine the meaning of the early episodes of a novel without reading it to the end.

The purpose of the universe, therefore, cannot be adequately stated from within our own situatedness. We are ourselves part of the canvas. We are characters in the story. We do not have the perspective whereby to give a final assessment of our own significance, or that of any phase of evolution, in the total scheme of things. We may in part understand the idea of God, however, as the cosmic artist or story-teller by whom the significance of every event and every life is guaranteed, though we cannot articulate exactly in what this significance consists.[32]

Our current attempts to understand the universe's untamed becoming in mutuality ultimately fail. There is something going on, which we want to know, but cannot quite grasp. As Whitehead sensed, we are actors in a cosmic mystery play and do not understand our role. Even those who profess the "death of God" sense some event is happening. Simon Critchley, the English Philosopher wrote recently that his beliefs seemed to be undergoing a shift, which he could not explain. At the end of the Introduction to his book *The Faith of the Faithless,* he concluded that the primary question for philosophy was no longer how to live; it was how to love. "Love is not just as strong as death—it is stronger." [33] This condition of being aware of something going on, in oneself and the cosmos, yet unable to know or grasp what it is epitomizes the mystery of human freedom in the universe for me.

We have barely become conscious in the twenty-first century that we are creating ourselves and, in some mysterious way, the universe. Like the astronauts in Clarke's novel, we have just "opened the door" on the awakening universe, and are beginning to try to understand our role in its becoming. It seems clear to me that each person's path to becoming authentically himself in the twenty-first century is increasingly connected with an awareness of and participation in this universal becoming in mutuality.

As we stand in awe, we cannot help but wonder where our Rama came from and why it was sent to us. There is a nagging sense that something is missing— or rather, that some presence has not yet been found. Where is the "coach" who is planning the game we are playing? Where is the "artist" who is shaping the beauty of the cosmos?

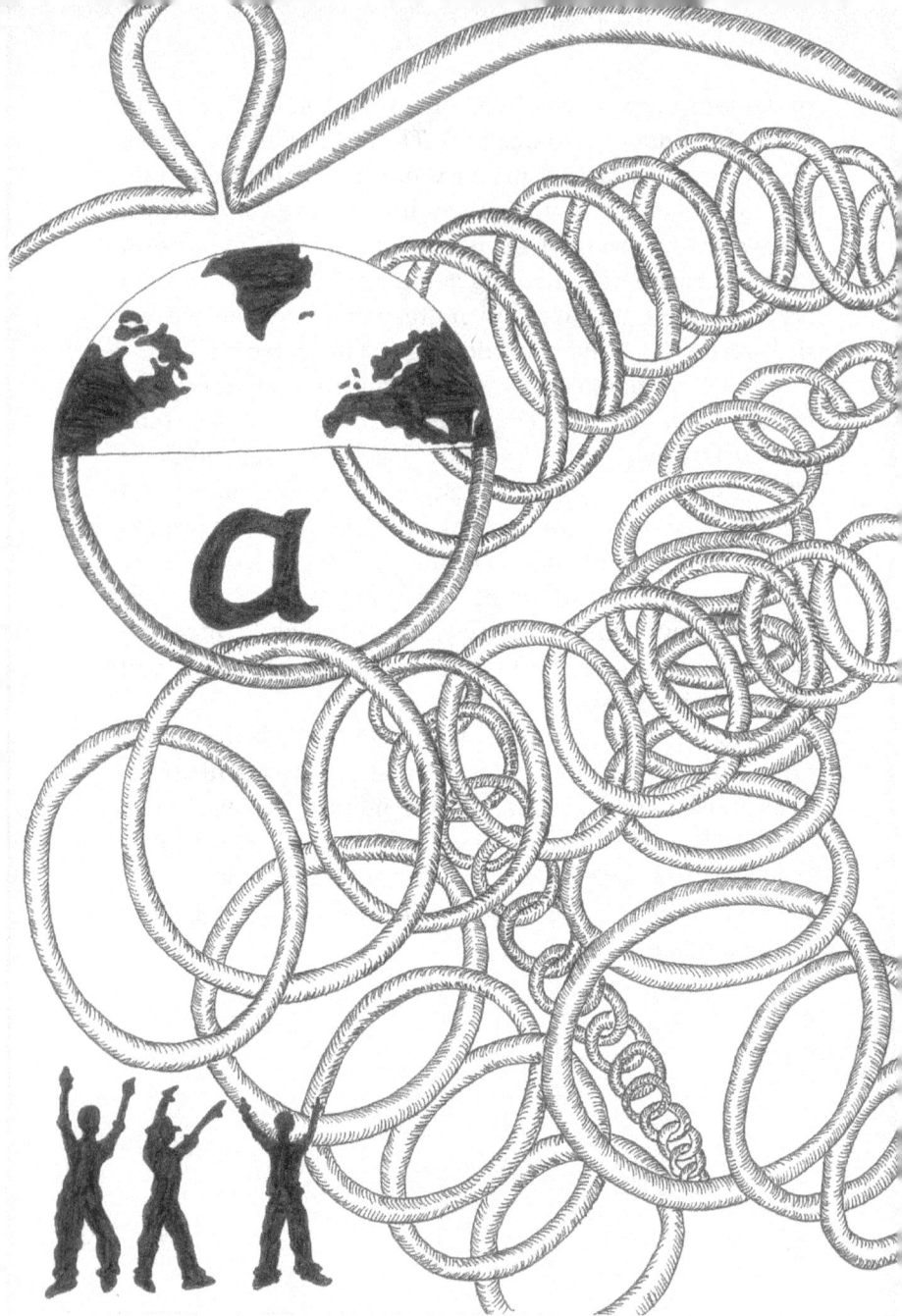

Figure 4—Untamed Becoming in Universal Mutuality

Chapter 6

THE ORIGIN AND DESTINY OF RAMA

Being is attempting to draw the entire created
order unto Itself, even with all its blockages
and resistances to such development.[34]
— William Schmidt

As Clarke's astronauts began to understand the marvels of the artificial world they had entered, they realized that some intelligence had built and sent Rama into the solar system. They tried to reason who these incredible beings might be; what far-away galaxy might be their home. They failed; there simply was not enough data inside the artificial world called Rama for them to reach any conclusions.

There are questions for which the data inside our universe are insufficient to form scientific theories. What exists, if anything, beyond space and time? Why does our cosmos exist at all? In what follows I imagine answers to these questions, which I will share with you. Your journey may be similar to mine or follow a different path altogether. Each person's journey has similarities and differences from everyone else's. As I said in the Preface, my hope is to awaken a desire in you to journey further into the unknown and decide for yourself—to converse with you, not convince you.

Mankind *is* inside our Rama. Our world inevitably shapes and limits us. "The mind is inherently embodied," as Professor of Linguistics George Lakoff states.[35] Still, we can imagine that our experience of Rama is not everything that exists. A common name that we give to the "is-ness" that is beyond space-time is "God". Different cultures have used different names—Yahweh, Allah, Bhagavan and many others—and, while respecting these holy names, I will use the English word God.[36]

God's reality is beyond the metaphors of human knowledge: an indescribable mystery, completely outside our experiences or concepts. God is beyond even the concepts of being and becoming we imagined in Chapters 4 and 5. Any metaphor we might use to imagine God hides more about God than it reveals. Therefore, we need an approach to the "is-ness that is beyond us" that does not directly try to imagine God. I will use a starting point suggested by the German theologian Karl Rahner. He starts with the "players" on the field (humanity) and not the "coach" or the "artist" (God) I imagined in previous chapters.[37]

An imaginative concept of man

Rahner states that only by imagining humanity in a fresh way can we hope to approach that which is beyond us. Put another way—if we start with the assumption that humanity is only an evolving, meaningless part of a meaningless universe, we have decided at the outset that no meaning beyond man exists. We cut ourselves off from other possibilities by this choice. Rahner's starting point is very different. He assumes that man is the central and essential component of all created existence, different from the rest of Rama in that man is a *transcendent being*. It is important to understand his concept of human transcendence, because it is the path Rahner follows to imagine God's game plan.

The observations of psychology, biochemistry, sociology, paleontology, and other sciences about mankind are largely valid. Yet—and this is the crux of Rahner's insight—no scientific theory can ever describe man in his totality because man is beyond Rama as well as part of Rama. Yes, man is a being whose origins appear to lie within the universe. But man also appears to go beyond, or transcend, this reality. Man *may* be more than a highly evolved member of the animal kingdom. Our mind may not just be some organic computer with software that will be eventually understood. This fundamental and irresolvable uncertainty about *what man is* points toward the possibility of human transcendence.

We most clearly experience this possibility when we question and doubt, not because we feel we are missing some needed facts about ourselves, but because we are curious about things that we can never quite reach. For thousands of years, probably since the dawn of human intelligence, man has asked questions about himself. The Psalmist asked, more than 3000 years ago, "What are human beings . . .?"[38] We quite often hide such deep questions from ourselves, about *what* we are as a human being. Nonetheless, the human unquenchable desire to know is always there. This lack of certainty about reality, which can never be adequately satisfied by our answers, is a sign pointing toward the possibility of our transcendence and is thus one of our greatest gifts.

We each start our personal exploration of what we believe from our own experiences. We can each decide if any of these experiences hint of transcendence, and are real and not just imagined. And if we hope that they are real, even if we are not convinced, then we can begin to believe—*in a initial, perhaps very tentative act of trust*—that a transcendent God may have made us also transcendent.[39]

Even if we are transcendent beings, we are also undeniably historical beings, living in time. Our lives and experiences are inseparable from the becoming of the universe. We are utterly dependent on our existence within the universe and are powerless to change this simple fact. We did not choose the cosmos in which we find ourselves, with all its difficulties and its wonder; yet we must choose how we live and act in this situation. In the final analysis, we cope with the historical situation into which we have been "thrown" as the philosopher Heidegger put it, while we also accept or deny our potential as transcendent persons. *We make this most basic choice in a decision of ultimate importance, trusting in our judgment.*

Man and indescribable mystery

When we allow ourselves to imagine that we may be transcendent, however tentatively we may sense it, and that God is utterly beyond our understanding and an indescribable mystery, then we have, in my opinion, established a starting point to imagine the game plan of the universe. Having once stated that God's mystery is infinitely beyond us, we can then imagine what it means for humanity to exist in the presence of absolute mystery.

This is a crucial point, involving our imagining the ultimate context for our life. What does my life mean? There are two possibilities we need to envision and compare. What does my life mean if God exists? And what does my life mean if nothing is "out there"? Is there a difference that is relevant to *my* life?

Human life in the presence of the indescribable mystery of God is radically different than our existence in the presence of nothingness (as some scientists and philosophers describe our situation). To imagine humanity in the presence of nothingness, we can read the German philosopher Friedrich Nietzsche:

> I beseech you, my brothers, *remain faithful to the earth*, and do not believe those who speak to you of otherworldly hopes! Poison-mixers are they, whether they know it or not. Despisers of life are they, decaying and poisoned themselves, of whom the earth is weary: so let them go.[40]

And:

> Do you know what 'the world' is to me?...a monster of energy, without beginning, without end,...that does not expend itself but only transforms itself,...enclosed by 'nothingness' as by a boundary...do you want a name for this world?... this world is the will to power—and nothing more. And you yourselves are also this will to power— and nothing besides.[41]

Nietzsche imagined that if man is only a highly evolved intelligent animal in an otherwise empty reality, then man is radically free to establish his own meaning. Australian Existential Psychotherapist Clare Mann describes this situation. "In an attempt to make sense of the infinite possibilities of life, we create myths or unquestioned assumptions which hoodwink us into believing there is an objective world." [42] Each person must create his or her own reality and live in it the best they can. As the French philosopher and writer Jean-Paul Sartre put it, "You are—your life, and nothing else." [43]

On the other hand, the transcendent starting point Rahner and I have imagined sees humanity existing in a completely different situation—in the presence of indescribable mystery. Mankind's freedom takes on a totally different meaning than the will to power and the ultimate emptiness of Nietzsche. Rather than man's will to power, we can imagine that we live in the presence of God's purpose for man.

We typically call what we are to become our "destiny," and since God has our ultimate purpose within a game plan, it liberates us in the sense that we are not forced to create our own ultimately empty destiny as Nietzsche described. The meaning and purpose of our lives exists outside us in God's indescribable mystery. But can we know our destiny (and God's game plan) if it is hidden in such impenetrable mystery?

We have already seen that mankind's scientific thinking, which is based purely on our physical senses, is incapable of penetrating beyond Rama. Even our transcendence, which we sense through original knowing, is only openness to the infinite and is not understanding. This is the deepest reality of man's situation: *we are inside Rama and unable to understand what is beyond Rama.* We cannot hope to know God like we know any other thing in existence. God is not an existent alongside all other existents. The ancient Hindus sensed this when they wrote in the Upanishads:

> The One Power . . . is the Ear behind the ears,
> Mind behind the mind, Speech behind speech,
> Vital Life behind life. The ears cannot hear it;
> it is what makes the ears hear. The eyes cannot
> see it; it is what makes the eyes see. You cannot
> speak about it; it is what makes you speak. The mind
> cannot imagine it; it is what makes the mind think. [44]

If we can hope to begin to grasp God's game plan and our destiny hidden in indescribable mystery it is only because God gives this capacity to us. And, as we have seen before, this capacity to know God and our destiny is always available, to some extent, to every human being in original knowing and our intuitions about reality. What finally emerges for us in reflection is that these hints of transcendence are gifts to us; *we are approached by indescribable mystery precisely because we cannot approach it.*

The historical reality of humanity seems to contradict this transcendent possibility. Perhaps Nietzsche was right after all—that man's will to power is his only destiny in this world. Maybe we "hoodwink" ourselves about having an ultimate destiny, and our transcendence is not real.

It does appear at first glance that humanity's transcendence has not had a significant impact on world history compared with mankind's will to power. But there are other possibilities. Perhaps God approached us once but now stays at a distance and simply watches us, biding his time. There is another possibility too—that God continues to approach us, but that we, in our freedom, choose not to respond. In either case, if we affirm that God has somehow approached humanity, then, if God is "good", the evil in human history results from our choices.[45] We are confronted by humanity's collective historical guilt in this possibility. Maybe that is why many people avoid thinking about this question.

In summary, each of us is faced with an ultimate choice: are we transcendent beings or not? This decision flows from what we imagine about God: the non-existence of God (nothingness), the existence of a remote God who created the universe yet stays at a distance (impersonal source of being) or a loving God mainly ignored by men (personal God).[46]

Continuing with the transcendent starting point, Rahner imagined God's game plan like this. "Man is the event of a free, unmerited and forgiving, and absolute self-communication of God." [47] Whatever you may think of humanity's responses to God throughout history—despite shocking human actions, even in the name of God—God continuously approaches us to radically transform each one of us. God's purpose and game plan is almost beyond belief—God wills to become our innermost reality, and transform what we are. This is transformation at the level of being and becoming—a time event, a breakthrough, of the divine into mankind's and the universe's deepest existence.

It is difficult to imagine what such transformation means, limited by our scientific concepts of reality and our everyday situation. Yet there are hints. Mystics throughout history have sensed its significance. Julian of Norwich, a fifteenth century Englishwoman said, "All shall be well, and all shall be well, and all manner of things shall be well." [48] We can hope that, even if we are not mystics, we too can sense the sweep and grandeur of God's transformative game plan in our own imagination, triggered by poetry, music, art and day-to-day experiences of friendship and unexpected goodness.

God's transformation of our lives happens in a time perspective that is very different than everyday time. The creative event of transformation happens now and not-now, and is like the flower always unfolding. We have already been given the divine gift in our being, and yet we await the completion of the gift. We live in the present, in the midst of cosmic becoming, so our human history has not yet fully responded to the gift that is at hand.

All of this is difficult to believe. If transcendence is real, why hasn't the human race shown more evidence of it? Yet, we can imagine that it is real. So what are we to do? That is the question I will address in the next chapter.

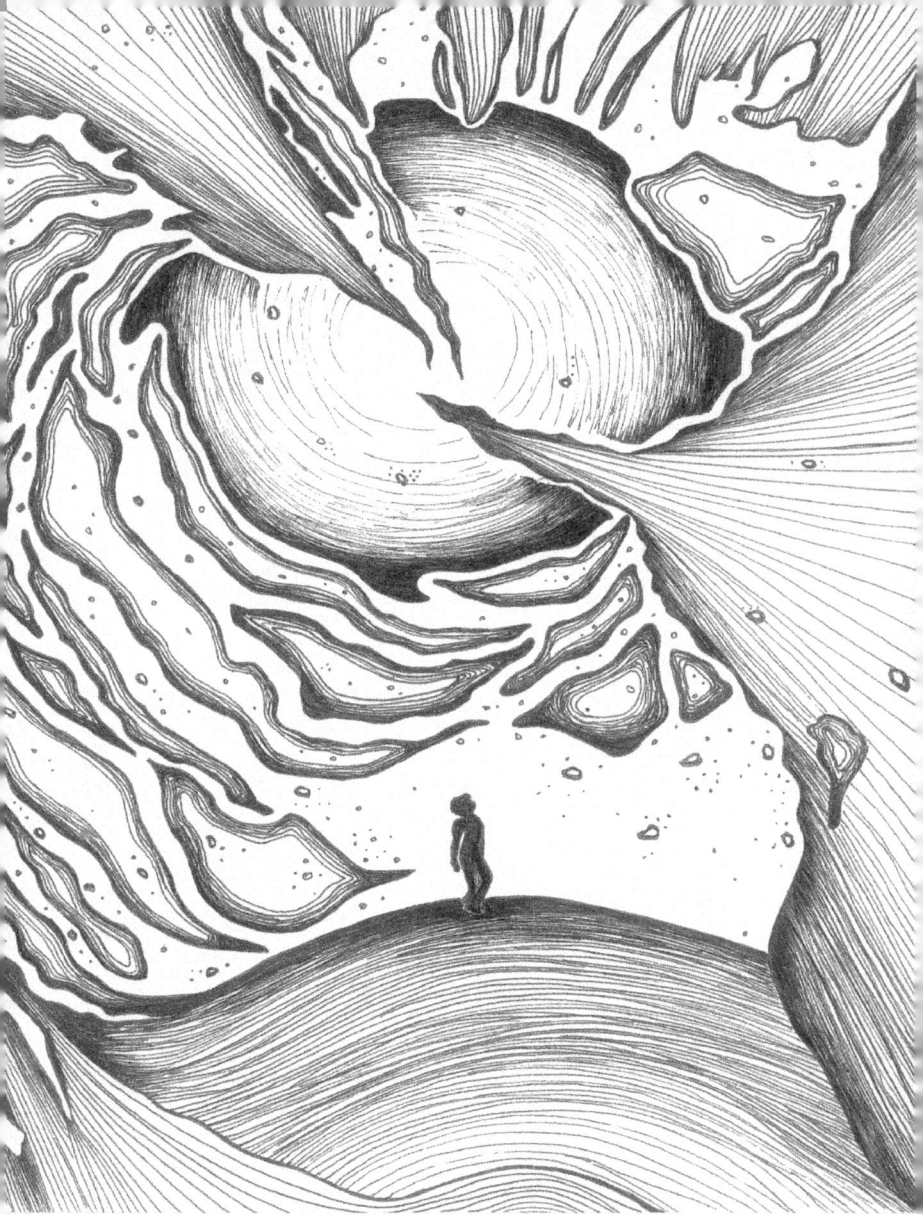

Figure 5—Transcendent Humanity

Chapter 7

TRUTH AND MEANING

The truth—that love is the ultimate and
the highest goal to which man can aspire.[49]
—Viktor Frankl

The gas chambers of Auschwitz, Treblinka,
and Maidanek were ultimately prepared not
in some ministry or other in Berlin, but
rather at the desks and in the lecture halls
of nihilistic scientists and philosophers.[50]
—Viktor Frankl

Our Rama is mysterious, and the idea of human transcendence is fascinating, but are these ideas true? And, even if they are true, what do they have to do with me? Why should I invest any time in pursuing such far out possibilities? What does all this mean, particularly to me?

These are questions that only you can answer. I can suggest how you might go about finding answers, but you have to *decide* to do the work. In the world of transforming organizations and mentoring in which I work, people generally need some significant motive before they invest time in seriously weighing and analyzing big decisions—a significant (to them) future promise or a personal "burning platform" problem in the present. That is also true for you when it comes to such ultimate questions.

No one can persuade you that you *must* engage in this journey any further; the motivation to continue this quest must come from within you. Still, let me cover some basic points about such a journey, or at least how it begins. Let me start with the question of truth and how it is linked to imagination.

Is what I imagine true?

There are so many shades of meaning of the word truth that we tend to slide easily from one idea about truth to another. There is the truth we learned as a child, which we must always tell, even if it hurts. "Did you take your sister's toy?" Either you did or you did not. You know the truth directly. There is courtroom truth. Is the evidence presented to the jury compelling? Did the person commit the crime? The jury never directly knows the truth about really happened because they were not present when the crime was committed. They have to rely on the testimony of witnesses and other evidence, and decide what the truth is, "beyond reasonable doubt." The judge defines precisely how the jury ought to decide whether or not they have reasonable doubts. The certain truth is only known by the accused.

There is the truth of mathematics. This partially consists of doing the math process correctly when solving an equation. However, even if the equation is correctly solved, the results may not fit reality. Meeting these two requirements describes the physicist's truth—using mathematics correctly and finding data through repeatable experiments to prove the equations fit external reality. However, while one may correctly create and solve equations, and find some data that fits, there is always the possibility that some new data and a better mathematical equation may exist, fitting reality better. Science is tentative about reality and truth, as I experienced at NASA and as we heard the Physicist Brian Green express previously.

Then there is philosophical truth, which is even more complex. All philosophies depend on a particular philosopher's starting assumptions about reality. Possibly the most well-known philosophical assumption of the modern era is "I think, therefore I am," made in the 17th century by Rene Descartes, a French mathematician and philosopher. Descartes assumed that human thinking (with its limitations) was at the center of his philosophy. His position has gradually evolved into a much broader (and more limiting) *scientific* statement about human thinking, summarized by Daniel Dennet, the Director for Cognitive Studies at Tufts University:

> "Of course our minds are our brains, and hence are just stupendously complex 'machines'; the difference between us and other animals is one of huge degree, not metaphysical kind . . .if human minds are nonmiraculous products of evolution, then they are artefacts and all their powers must have an ultimately 'mechanical' explanation." [51]

I will henceforth call this assumption the "Brain-centric" assumption or stance about human knowing. In the Brain-centric assumption, human thinking and ideas and truth are separate from reality. Ideas are "inside" the human mind and reality is "outside". How does one link the images and concepts in our minds with the reality that may or may not exist outside our minds? There has never been a satisfactory answer to this philosophical question in the Brain-centric stance, starting with Descartes right up to the present.[52] Furthermore, as we have seen, science and mathematics are tentative and can never completely describe reality, only approximate it. That leaves people in the Brain-centric stance uncertain of what human beings can know, and lays the ground work for the ambiguities of postmodernism. As the American scholar Richard Tarnas wrote, "The one postmodern absolute is critical consciousness which, by deconstructing all, seems compelled by its own logic to do so to itself as well. This is the unstable paradox that permeates the postmodern mind." [53] In my opinion, the Brain-centric assumption which puts the human mind and science at the center of its philosophy has found its way into a dead-end.

Descartes statement "I think, therefore I am" may be widely known today, but actually it is just one possible assumption about reality. Another assumption is "Things including me exist, therefore I think." Aristotle and others assumed that reality ("what is"), including being itself, is at the center of their philosophy. The human "intellect" is equipped to directly know the cosmos's reality, at least to some degree, not only through science but in many other ways as well. As I have stated previously, however, even though reality exists external to us, we still need to test that our personal imagination, insights and ideas "fit" with that reality. I will discuss how we accomplish that a bit later. Henceforth I will call this other philosophical stance the "Reality-centric" assumption.[54]

Why am I leading you through this somewhat complicated discussion about philosophical assumptions? Because, at the heart of every person's search for authenticity lies their own (probably implicit) fundamental assumption about reality. Generally speaking, in our modern period, many people hold the assumption that "Truth is *only* what I decide it is, in my own mind." That is a very different assumption than the truth about "what is" lies outside oneself—and that one must engage in a serious "quest for truth." It seems important to understand the implications of these two different assumptions if a person seeks to be authentic and true to herself.[55]

So how does the quest for truth about our Rama and its possibilities work? Suppose you have some imaginative insight about reality, like the ones in this book for example. In the Reality-centric stance, you do not spend time examining whether you can know reality or not, as many modern philosophers do. You assume you can know it—your human intellectual capacity is built-in—so you proceed immediately to examine the insight itself, to see whether it matches reality or not. Reality *may* include the expansive views of time, space, consciousness and the "game plan" of the cosmos discussed earlier. Such intuitions are true if they reasonably fit with reality, which is both "what is" and "what is not yet but what might be". The question of truth in the Reality-centric stance becomes, how do you verify if your imaginative insight fits "what is" in reality?

Bernard Lonergan in his book *Insight* uses the term "position" to describe how one either uses the full weight of human wisdom to decide whether something is true, or one merely glances or "looks" at the question. In exploring how one would seriously pursue the truth of an insight, not simply "glance at it," he describes human knowing as both multi-faceted (polymorphic) and common to all humans (isomorphic). Polymorphic simply refers to the commonsense notion that we know different things in different ways. For example, there are obvious differences between knowing mathematically and knowing poetically, knowing that someone loves you, or knowing a painting is beautiful. Because we know different aspects of reality differently, we must employ different ways of testing the "fit" of our insights based on what we are dealing with. You cannot use mathematics to decide whether your wife truly loves you, or whether you are truly a transcendent person.

I want to focus, however, on the Isomorphic dimension of knowing that Lonergan describes. Basically, this means that *all* human beings possess the same built-in intellectual capacity to process their insights and determine if these intuitions are reasonable "fits" with reality. In the Reality-centric stance, truth resides outside the human mind in reality itself. We need not worry about that. What Lonergan says we must do—and are equipped to do—is (1) trust our drive to know and our experiences of reality, (2) recognize and clarify our intuitions about the patterns and significance of these experiences, and (3) make judgments about the reasonableness and "fit" of our insights with the truth in reality.[56] These three steps are Lonergan's description of the fundamental cognitional or knowing process present in every human being. They also help us decide how to act.

Let me give you a few examples of how Lonergan's knowing process works. I was once taking the square root of a large number using a paper-and-pencil method I learned in grammar school—what number multiplied by itself will yield the given large number? As I did the repetitive steps to get the answer, I saw a pattern in the steps and had an insight. I realized that I could alter this manual process in a simple way and make it work for the cube root or, in fact any root of any number! (What number multiplied by itself three times, or four times, or 'n' times yields the given number?) I tried the cube root steps and it worked. Then the fourth root and that worked. Eureka! I had discovered something.

You can see Lonergan's steps in this example. (1) My experience was paying attention to the steps of the process for taking the square root, not just doing it automatically and not paying attention. (2) My insight was noticing the repetitive pattern and realizing instinctively that it could be extended to the cube or any root. (3) My judgment of the correctness of my insight was trying the steps for the cube and fourth roots and seeing that they worked. Afterwards, I surveyed the need for such a manual process realizing that, with computers, people could find the roots of numbers far easier that my manual method, and decided to do nothing further.

Another example comes from my mentoring experiences. Once I was coaching a woman entrepreneur who had difficulties with time management. I asked her to list all the things she had to do in a week, and she came up with a long list. (1) I read her list and (2) *noticed a pattern in the list:* some things were actual work she had to do, some things were deciding which work she should do, and some things were about researching which tasks were important strategically. I had an *insight* that these three patterns corresponded to three different roles that she was playing in her one-person company: worker, manager and executive.

I asked her how she decided which role to be in during the day and she did not think about those roles or plan her time in that way. It was as if there was no manager in her company assigning work; her worker role just did everything on the list. In her executive role she was worried whether these tasks contributed to her business success but there was no manager to carry out her desire to stop doing less valuable tasks. Thinking explicitly about these three roles gave her a way to better manage her time and create success. Based on her response, (3) I *judged* that there was value in my insight and afterwards decided to include this way of thinking in my consulting practice from that point forward. I think you can see how Lonergan's cognitive process worked in this case.

Now let me walk you through one of the insights I have described in the previous chapter—man is a transcendent being. How might Lonergan's process work in this case? (1) There are *experiences* that we notice: questions we cannot answer, feelings of connection to the cosmos, poetic emotions, etc. Or we might be "carried away" by a piece of music or the beauty of a sunset. (2) We might notice a *pattern* in these—that all these experiences are open-ended, and we cannot imagine any way to ever get to the bottom of why they happen or how they work. We might have an *insight* that these experiences are common to all men and women, and point toward an unlimited capacity to know that purely biological processes apparently cannot explain. (3) Then we could undertake some study to see whether other people have had similar experiences and insights, and find a wealth of sources (including Karl Rahner's works). This would help us make a *judgment* that our insight reasonably fits with reality. Afterwards, having discovered the reasonableness of our potential transcendence, we might decide to implement certain changes in our life, eg, find a community of like minded people who have made the same discovery, get engaged in activities which help transform the world, etc.

These examples show how a person with the Reality-centric assumption might approach such questions. To the Brain-centric stance, the mathematical and mentoring examples I used would probably raise no philosophical questions about reality, but the transcendent example clearly does. The Brain-centric stance would approach the question of human transcendence very differently. Such people might notice the same phenomena—questions we cannot answer, feelings of connection to the cosmos, poetic emotions, etc. However, because of their assumption that human thinking is the measure of truth, the Brain-centric person would try to explain where such phenomena and thoughts about them originated in the evolved human brain. It might be in certain connections in the brain, or culturally induced emotions from a person's life experiences, or other causes. The Brain-centric conclusion might then be, given that we can explain these occurrences by some organic thinking process in the human mind, satisfying some natural survival of the fittest condition, we do not need any further explanation.

The ultimate Brain-centric conclusion might be that human beings have no way of knowing for certain whether they are transcendent or not, and that terms like transcendent (or God for that matter) are purely speculative, not verifiable by scientific methods, and therefore meaningless. The Brain-centric assumption about knowing, in a nut shell, is how some people in the modern world might reason their way to the atheist position or the "death of God." [57]

To summarize, I believe that each person has an implicit stance that probably resembles either the Brain-centric or Reality-centric stance. In their pursuit of authenticity, each person ought to examine whatever assumption they are making and decide whether it is the one they wish to hold. How can you do that? My suggestion is to start with a commonsense approach. Ask yourself, based on my examples, using Lonergan's knowing process: (1) What is my experience about which stance or assumption that I lean toward? Do the implications of the Reality-centric or the Brain-centric stance resonate more strongly with me? Is there some other stance that I generally use? (See Table 1 at the end of this chapter for a brief summary of the Brain-centric versus Reality-centric stances and some of their implications). (2) See if you have any intuitions about which stance you sense may be true. I would suggest simply noting your feelings and intuitions at this point, and not trying to take step (3) and judge whether they make sense or not, or deciding what you want to do. Read the rest of the book. Make that judgment later or continue your study about which assumption you will use to reach the truth of reality in your search for authenticity.

If my insights are true, what is their meaning to me?

This is very much like a standard "change" question, which I encounter in my mentoring practice. If I have insights about myself and the world, which imply different future possibilities, what do they mean to me? Do I need to change? With my clients, I break this question down into two parts. First motivation. You must clarify your understanding of the future and the outcome that you desire. That is the question I will focus on. The second question, which I will not cover, is what steps should I follow to realize the outcome I desire? I will leave this question for your future consideration, after you finish reading this book, to be reflected upon and discussed with people you trust. At the end of this chapter, I will make a recommendation for a starting point for this journey toward your desired future for your consideration.

Generally people say they want a brighter, happier future as an outcome, which is good as far as it goes. The key to establishing strong motivation, however, is to get a very clear understanding of how you will *experience* a brighter, happier future once you have arrived. It should be obvious by now that the imaginative insights into the reality of Rama that we discussed earlier in the book—time, space, consciousness, freedom and transcendence—create a very different "horizon" for experiencing the future. If man is a transcendent being, this means that the future he will experience is both within our current space-time *and* beyond it, in what many commonly call "eternity". This is a very different future than many self-help books promise, which focus on skill development, problem solving or "getting what will make you happy" right now. While these may be quite useful as outcomes, they may not be the primary outcome of interest to a transcendent person, who has a different time horizon and context for their life.

What does the future mean to me? If we are a transcendent person then meaning is both something that we are conscious of as well as something beyond us. We are conscious of the significance of some of the implications of our freedom but not all. As we saw before, we are aware of something going on, in ourselves and the cosmos, yet we unable to know or grasp completely what it is. Each person, ultimately, must seek his own insights into these things, but to help you understand how you might experience your own journey as a transcendent person, consider the following two stories.

Two Transcendent Stories

Most people have seen George Lucas's masterpiece *Star Wars*. In Episode IV (the first movie), Luke Skywalker, a young man, is living with his uncle and aunt on a remote farm on a distant planet. His life is hum-drum, but then he meets old Ben Kenobi, a strange hermit living in the desert. Ben tells Luke that he knew his father—who Luke believes is dead—and that he was a Jedi Knight. Once Luke discovers that he is the son of a Jedi Knight, he becomes restless and wants to leave his uncle's farm. In a scene of great dramatic impact, as dusk is falling, we see Luke standing by himself, looking out at the distant horizon, with a magnificent musical theme swelling. We can feel with Luke what it means to discover that everything in life is about to change. If you watch this scene again on DVD, you will notice that it marks the boundary between the old "everyday" Luke and the new "transcendent" Luke. His journey toward his destiny begins here.

The second story is my own experience. First a little background. I was raised in the Roman Catholic Church and was faithful to its beliefs. I went to Catholic and public schools and Jesuit universities. I married a young woman I met at university and we had two children. Like many men of that era (the 1960s and 1970s), I soon began to devote most of my energies to becoming successful. Success became my "god." I kept going to church but God was kept in a small "box" that I only opened for an hour on Sunday.

In the early 1980s, I had become a Vice President of a company and felt that all my work had paid off. But then "the wheels came off." The company was acquired by another company and I was no longer on the top of the heap.

Coincidently, at the same time, a good friend of mine, a devout Baptist named Henry, invited me to come to a monthly breakfast, where five men from our company read selections from spiritual works and discussed what they meant to us. My concept of God at the time was that he was "up there," remote from us, not really involved in our lives. But as I listened to Henry, he talked about God as if he were right here, an intimate friend that was helping him in his daily life. The difference in our viewpoints nagged at me for a few months.

One Saturday morning, as I was eating breakfast, something occurred to me. If God really was present as Henry said, then I could ask him to show me his presence.

I said what was probably the deepest most heart-felt prayer of my life: "God, if it is possible, please show me yourself and help me. I am so miserable." Then I waited.

Nothing happened on that Saturday or for several weeks. Then one day after work I was reading the Reader's Digest, a popular monthly magazine. In the front was a short first person account by a woman who had encountered God in her life. She had decided that God was like a doctor. When you were sick, you went and sat in the doctor's office and, after awhile, he came out. She did that, sitting quietly each day, and God eventually came out of his "office" and helped her. That was it! I would do the same thing.

Very early, before dawn the next morning, I crept downstairs and sat in my living room, which I imagined was God's waiting room. I sat there quietly with a Bible on my lap and read a passage (I forget which one) then just waited. Even today I get choked up when I tell this story. God came out of his office and touched me. I felt a warmth around me (it was a cold February morning) and clearly heard in my mind, "I love you just as you are Jim." I experienced God's unconditional love, which, for someone who was judging himself a failure, was like being rescued from a dark hole in the ground. From that moment until the present, I have known like Henry, that God is always present, whether I or anyone else senses that. That experience was the one I referred to in the Preface and it changed my life. Not that I was instantly transformed, but I set off on a path, led by God, that eventually opened up new possibilities, including writing this book. This may all sound impossible to you but I know it happened and speak with confidence about what God is doing in my life.

My quest is seeking the truth of what is "out there". My problem before that February encounter with God was that I focused on myself and my own success not what was out there—my wife, my children, others and especially God. My breakthrough came when I admitted that to myself and opened myself to receiving help. I am still on a journey, of understanding what it means to be a transcendent person, trying to open myself more, to others and God, and to understand my role in creating the future.

Your transcendent story

What can I recommend, now that you have come this far with me? I am not a "guru." I do not have my own patented secret of life, and this is not a book about "10 Easy Steps to Achieve Transcendence." I want to help you to see your life as a story.

I am a great believer in story-telling. It is a fundamental human capability. Everyone enjoys and instinctively tells stories. We not only communicate better using stories but we also learn the significance of what we have experienced when we describe what happened to us as a story. A story has a plot—a beginning, middle and end. The characters in a story do not act mindlessly; they have roles to play in the plot. Stories are containers of meaning.

The great stories (myths) have continuing significance over thousands of years. Joseph Campbell wrote of the hero myths common in most human cultures in *The Hero with a Thousand Faces*. Jesus used timeless stories (parables), which still communicate his meaning after 2000 years. Rollo May, in *The Cry for Myth*, said that "Myth is an eternal truth in contrast to an empirical truth. The latter can change with every morning newspaper, when we read of the latest discoveries in our laboratories. But the myth transcends time" [58]

So, to tell your story is to make sense of the deeper, mythical meaning of your life and, in a sense, transcend time. But how can you tell your story in such a powerful way?

Many years ago I wrote down the story of my own life. I wrote about the future mainly, not trying to analyze the causes of how I got to where I was. I used an allegory about a man (me) who was lost but then encountered, like Luke Skywalker, something that launched him into a great adventure. What I did in the story was take myself out of ordinary time to see my life as a growing event in the future, which I could look down on and see with a "god-like" perspective. The interesting thing is, many years later, when I reread my story, it still has meaning for me. The event of my life is still growing like I imagined. That gives me a sense of peace somehow.

It is important to be truthful in your own imaginative future life story—and that is really the only reason to write it—so you must write truthfully about the "big questions of life"—love, personal growth, death and "what it all means". This will inevitably bring you face to face with how you view the reality of transcendence. As you tell your story, the character (you) in the story just acts according to how you see truth, as you experience the imaginative events of your future life.

Telling the future story of your life may seem difficult. You may feel that you cannot write well enough. The only one who needs to read what you write, and to whom it has to make sense is you. And that is the whole point. Your life has to make sense to you; that is what people mean when they say we must live "authentically." Telling yourself the story of your future life is a great way to hold up a mirror to yourself and find out whether you are living (or intend to live) the future life you desire.

Here are a few hints about how to get started writing your story. They all involve getting above the timeline of your life, and observing what happens in the future.

> 1. When I wrote my life story, I jotted down the first two sentences and then let the rest flow from my imagination. The sentences were—"Halfway through my life I encountered a mysterious place. I found it, or to be truthful it found me, as I was beginning a long planned vacation, by myself." These sentences established that I encountered something that would change my life. I just listened to my imagination about what happened after that and wrote it down.
>
> 2. The Author Charles Handy suggested another approach. "When you get to heaven, you will meet the person you might have been." [59] What did this person accomplish? Whom did this person love? What differences did this person make in her or his family? Community? The world? Let your transcendent story imagine, feel, envision this person you want to be. Then describe how you got to be that person, starting from where you are now.
>
> 3. Imagine you are at a testimonial dinner in your honour after having retired from a long and successful career. Imagine your best friends are telling anecdotes and stories about you. What will they say about you—your accomplishments, your loves, the lives you touched, the gifts you shared? Then imagine you leave the dinner and describe what happens next, after you leave the dinner.

Those are just three ideas. The important thing is to find a way that works for you. I suggest that you not go back to the past and try to explain how you got where you are. You story is not self-analysis or explaining what happened, up to the present. I encourage you to start with who you are and what your situation is, right now, and go forward.

So that is my recommendation. Tell your future life story to yourself. See if what you imagine might happen to you. My advice is to write a happy ending to your story!

Life is but life, and death but death!
Bliss is but bliss, and breath but breath!
And if, indeed, I fail
At least to know the worst is sweet. [60]

BRAIN-CENTRIC STANCE	REALITY-CENTRIC STANCE
"I think, therefore I am" (Descartes and many modern philosophers).	"Things exist, therefore I think" (Aristotle and some modern philosophers).
Only what human thinking can validate scientifically can be known with any certainty. Everything else is speculation.	Human knowing, including original knowing, can experience many different aspects of reality and validate these insights into reality.
Man is only what science can validate: an animal with a highly developed intelligence and self-consciousness.	Man is a mystery to man, a being with a spiritual dimension, which science can never validate.
God is an unnecessary hypothesis. Science will ultimately be able to explain everything, even how the universe created itself.	God exists and has created man as a transcendent being, different than everything else in the universe.
There is a conflict between science and religion. Science knows the truth and religion is an out dated way of thinking.	There is no conflict between science (which knows certain physical aspects of reality) and religion (which knows other non-physical aspects of reality).
Each person possesses their own relative truth and meaning, which they must create for themselves.	Truth and meaning exist outside man's mind but man can reach them, including insights into God's mystery, with God's help.
Man has no destiny. Each person must ultimately rely on himself to realise success in this life.	Man has a purpose and destiny created by God and must ultimately depend on God to fully realise these, in this life and eternity.

Table 1: Some Implications of the Brain-centric
and Reality-centric Stances

Conclusion

What can I say at the end of this brief journey to the hard-working single mom or father, or the struggling entrepreneur I described in the Preface?

Congratulations, first of all, for sticking with the journey. Some of the ideas I covered are not easy; you may have had to work a bit to understand them. Your effort in the journey will be worth it if you begin to see the context for your life as hopeful, full of potential and, most important, intimately linked to the universal game plan. While I believe that this is the reality of *every* human life, your own confidence and peacefulness about this is what is important.

You explored a vital question as you read this book—what do you imagine about reality? You must ultimately decide whether what you imagine is *truly* real, in a personally unique journey within your own depths. In a way, this journey has already begun. So, write your life story and tell it to people you love and trust, to help you see more clearly what your destiny is, and where God is leading you.

My sense of human destiny is that, in the creative embrace of time, each of us is becoming infinitely more than we are at present through a transforming process orchestrated by God. My belief is that mankind has already been given this gift in history through the entrance of the deepest reality of God into mankind's being. Each of us, in freedom, accepts or rejects this gift, which is constantly offered to each of us in diverse ways. In freedom, we can choose to actively participate in God's game plan to transform the rest of the universe into infinite transcendence. Our too ordinary assessment of our value and the worth of our human actions block our wholehearted participation in this transforming process.

The gift of transcendence that we have been given is marvelous beyond all human comprehension. My hope is that everyone who reads this book will trust enough in the incredible kindness of God to empty themselves of what stands in the way of their transformation. Emptying ourselves opens us to more fully realize the meaning of our transcendence. After reflecting on our true personal worth, we are enabled to humbly serve God in the creation of universal mutuality and transcendence. This is the context for life that I referred to in the Preface.

No person can "self-help" themselves into knowing God. That, as we have seen, is a gift. As a metaphor, Luke Skywalker needed the Force but had to learn to let go, taught by the Jedi Master Yoda. In a similar way, as I related in my story, I had to let go and go sit in God's "waiting room," to encounter what was beyond me. That is the only guidance I can give you. As the Psalmist said 3000 years ago, "Be still and know that I am God." [61]

Further Reading

If you would like to read more about the ideas explored in this book, I recommend starting with some of the following books.

A good place to start

Girzone, Joseph. *Joshua*. New York, Touchstone, 2003.

Hesse, Hermann. *Siddhartha*. New York, Bantam, 1971.

Purcell, Brendan. *From Big Bang to Big Mystery,* Veritas, Dublin, 2011.

Tarnas, Richard. *The Passion of the Western Mind*. New York, Ballantine Books, 1991.

Next step

Berry, Thomas. *The Great Work*. New York, Belltower, 1999.

Carroll, John. *The Western Dreaming*. Sydney, HarperCollins, 2001.

Collins, Francis S. *The Language of God*. New York, Free Press, 2006.

Houghton, Rosemary. *The Passionate God*. New York, Paulist Press, 1981.

Kung, Hans. *On Being a Christian*. New York, Image Books, 1984.

Selman, Francis. *Aquinas 101*. Notre Dame IN, Ave Maria Press, 2007.

Smith, Huston. *The World's Religions: Our Great Wisdom Tradition*. New York, HarperOne, 1958, rev. ed. 1991.

More depth

Armstrong, Karen. *The Great Transformation*. New York, Borzoi Books, 2006.

Coles, Robert. *The Secular Mind*. Princeton NJ, Princeton University Press, 1999.

Dennett, Daniel. *Consciousness Explained*. Boston, Little, Brown & Company, 1991.

Dennett, Daniel. *Darwin's Dangerous Idea*. New York, Simon & Schuster, 1995.

Gallagher, Michael Paul. *Faith Maps*. New York, Paulist Press, 2010.

Greene, Brian. *The Fabric of the Cosmos*. New York, W. W. Norton, 2004.

James, William. *The Varieties of Religious Experience*. New York, Touchstone, 1997.

Kung, Hans. *Does God Exist?*. New York, Vintage Books, 1981.

Kung, Hans. *Islam: Past, Present and Future*. New York, Crossroad, 2007.

Kung, Hans. *Judaism: Between Yesterday and Tomorrow*. New York, Crossroad, 1992.

Maguire, Daniel. *The Moral Core of Judiasm and Christianity*. Minneapolis, Fortress Press, 1993.

Difficult, but seminal

Braman, Brian J. *Meaning and Authenticity*. Toronto, University of Toronto Press, 2008.

Gilson, Etienne. *Methodical Realism*. San Francisco, Ignatius Press, 1990.

Lonergan, Bernard, S.J. *Insight*. New York, Longmans, 1958.

Maritain, Jacques. *Creative Intuition in Art and Poetry*. New York, Meridian Books, 1955.

Rahner, Karl S.J. *The Foundations of Christian Faith*. New York, Crossroad, 1978.

Steiner, George. *After Babel*. Oxford, Oxford University Press, 1998.

Appendix
SCINTILLA

Scintilla: a minute amount; trace; from the Latin *spark*

The following texts are presented as an additional source of reflective material to help you sense your own intuitions of reality and the context for your life.

I recommend reading each of them and trying to sense what hints about transcendence they trigger in you. Do not worry if nothing emerges. Poetry may not be your "thing."

"Dirge in Woods" by George Meredith

A wind sways the pines,
  And below
Not a breath of wild air;
Still as the mosses that glow
On the flooring and over the lines
Of the roots here and there.
The pine-tree drops its dead;
They are quiet, as under the sea.
Overhead, overhead
Rushes life in a race,
As the clouds the clouds chase;
  And we go,
And we drop like the fruits of the tree,
  Even we,
  Even so.[62]

"Buddha in Glory" by Rainer Maria Rilke

Center of all centers, core of cores,
almond self-enclosed, and growing sweet—
all this universe, to the furthest stars
all beyond them, is your flesh, your fruit.

Now you feel how nothing clings to you;
your vast shell reaches into endless space,
and there the rich, thick fluids rise and flow.
Illuminated in your infinite peace,

a billion stars go spinning through the night,
blazing high above your head.
But in you is the presence that
will be, when all the stars are dead.[63]

From "The Ascent of Mount Carmel"
by Saint John of the Cross

In the happy night,
In secret, when none saw me,
Nor I beheld aught,
Without light or guide, save that which burned
in my heart.

This light guided me
More surely than the light of noonday,
To the place where he (well I knew who!)
was awaiting me
—A place where none appeared.

Oh, night that guided me,
Oh, night more lovely than the dawn,
Oh, night that joined Beloved with lover,
Lover transformed in the Beloved! [64]

From The Book of Proverbs

Wisdom cries aloud in the street:
in the markets she raises her voice;
on top of the walls she cries out;
at the entrance of the city gates she speaks:
"How long, O simple ones, will you love being simple?"

The Lord created me at the beginning of his work,
the first of his acts of old.
Ages ago I was set up...
when he marked out the foundations of the earth,
then I was beside him, like a master workman;
and I was daily his delight,
rejoicing before him always,
rejoicing in his inhabited world
and delighting in the sons of men.

And now, my sons, listen to me:
happy are those who keep my ways...
but he who misses me injures himself;
all who hate me love death.[65]

"You, You Only, Exist" by Rainer Maria Rilke

You, you only, exist.
We pass away, till at last,
our passing is so immense
that you arise: beautiful moment,
in all your suddenness,
arising in love, or enchanted
in the contraction of work.

To you I belong, however time may
wear me away. From you to you
I go commanded. In between
the garland is hanging in chance; but if you
take it up and up and up: look:
all becomes festival! [66]

The Illustrations

Figure 1: Rama and Earth
The reader is one of the astronauts sent to investigate the strange object entering the solar system (and her life). You are looking out the porthole of the spaceship you are on as you approach the huge cylindrical object, with Earth and the stars in the background.

Figure 2: The Events and Blooming of Time
The Events and Strangeness of Time is shown by the petals of a flower opening, with the Big Bang and chaos in the center creating time. The reader is participating in time as an event herself.

Figure 3: Being, Space and Consciousness
The two main layers of human reality are shown. At the top, in a very thin layer, is *experienced sensory reality* (everyday). The main part of the picture is the deeper layer accessible to the imagination as *insightful reality*. You can see aspects of insightful reality in the main part of the illustration. The mathematical equation is one depiction of Calabi-Yau, which is physics' current best view of a unifying theory of everything. The netting structure represents philosophy's deepest insight called being, which underlies everything. The symbols at the bottom, in a darker layer, represent man's insights into the mystery beyond Rama, with "Alpha and Omega" representing the Judeo-Christian insight and the "Om" symbol representing the Buddhist insight. The reader has climbed down below the experienced sensory reality into insightful reality to explore what is there.

Figure 4: Untamed Becoming in Universal Mutuality
The reader experiences the untamed freedom of reality to become anything, in the dancing figures at the bottom. The wild strands of reality are swirling but the Earth is also being unveiled. At the top of the figure is Omega, the end toward which everything is going. The Alpha inside the emerging Earth is the game plan, which is the universal mutuality that being is bringing everything toward the Omega point.

Figure 5: Transcendent Humanity
The figure (and the reader) stands in awe of the insight that they and all humanity are being made transcendent by the same "wind that awakened the stars" (W. B. Yeats).

Notes

1 William Butler Yeats, Maid Quiet,
http://www.poemhunter.com/poem/maid-quiet/
2 Suzanne Langer, Philosophy in a New Key
(Cambridge, MA, Harvard University Press, 1993), 270
3 New International Version of the Bible, Acts of the Apostles 2:17
4 William B. Macomber, Anatomy of Disillusion,
Martin Heidegger's notion of truth
(Chicago, IL, Northwestern University Press, 1967)
5 William Shakespeare, A Midsummer Night's Dream, V, i
6 Carol Joyce Oates at World Science Festival 2012, quoted on
Readers Almanac, the official blog of The Library of America,
http://blog.loa.org/2012/06/joyce-carol-oates-and-jeffrey-
eugenides.html
7 Karl Rahner, Foundations of Christian Faith
(New York, NY, Crossroad Publishing Company, 1978), 18
8 Jacques Maritain, Creative Intuition in Art and Poetry,
Meridian Books, New York, 1955
9 St Augustine, Confessions.
10 Albert Einstein, quoted on San Diego State University,
Department of Psychology,
http://www-rohan.sdsu.edu/ ~ jconte/QuotesOnTime.html
11 Alvin Toffler, Future Shock
(New York, NY, Bantam Books, 1970), 15.
12 Ranier Maria Rilke, from The Ninth Elegy, in The Duino
Elegies, http://www.hunterarchive.com/files/Poetry/Elegies/
elegy9.html
13 Martin Heidegger, http://www.goodreads.com/author/
quotes/6191.Martin_Heidegger?auto_login_attempted = true
14 Described by the Calabi-Yau Manifold in superstring theory .
Actually, the latest estimate of dimensions is now 11.
Calabi-Yau manifolds have 9 dimensions and M-Theory adds
one more, which, including the dimension of time makes 11
dimensions instead of 10.
15 Abraham Maslow, Toward a Psychology of Being
(New York, NY, John Wiley & Sons, 1968)

[16]   The Gaia Hypothesis, which sees Earth as a holist
community of organisms cooperating to make the planet
habitable, advanced by scientists such as Teilhard de
Chardin and more recently by James Lovelock has not
received wide support in the scientific community.

[17]   Stephen Hawking, A Brief History of Time
(London, Bantam Press, 1998), p. 190

[18]   William Blake,
http://www.poemhunter.com/poem/auguries-of-innocence/

[19]   William Schmidt, "An Ontological Model of Development."
Journal of Pastoral Care 40, no. 1 (1986): 56-67

[20]   The family of beings that humans are most closely related to,
the hominids, began to emerge on our Rama about 7,000,000
years ago. If the timeline from the Big Bang to the present day
were equivalent to one of our days, the hominids would emerge
in the last minute of that day. Our own human history would be
equivalent to the last second of that minute. It is certainly fair to
say that we have "just landed" on our Rama.

[21]   There is a third choice but it doesn't seem a plausible one
to me. The universe (and human actions) could be completely
predetermined. In this view, free will is a myth humans
construct to avoid the implications of their situation.

[22]   Richard Feynman, The Meaning of It All
(London, The Penguin Press, 1998), 23

[23]   New International Version of the Bible, Letter to the Romans 7:15

[24]   To understand more about the God particle go to wikipedia
article on the Higgs Boson; for the Grand Theory of Everything
go to wikipedia article on the Grand Unified Theory

[25]   Brian Greene, The Fabric of the Cosmos
(New York, NY, Vintage Books, 2004)

[26]   Greene.

[27]   Dylan Thomas, The Force that through the Green Fuse
Drives the Flower, from Collected Poems of Dylan Thomas
1934 – 1953 (New York, NY, New Directions, 1971)

[28]   Karen Armstrong, The Great Transformation
(New York, NY, Alfred A Knopf, 2006), 378.

[29]   Rabbi Hillel,from Karen Armstrong, The Case for God
(New York, Anchor, 2010), 83.

[30] New International Version of the Bible, Gospel of Luke 6:31

[31] Teilhard de Chardin SJ, Hymn of the Universe
(New York, NY, Harper & Row, 1961)

[32] Ted and Winnie Brock in Religion Online; http://www.
religion-online.org/showchapter.asp?title = 1948&C = 1815

[33] Simon Critchley, The Faith of the Faithless
(London, Verso, 2012)

[34] Schmidt

[35] George Lakoff and Mark Johnson, Philosophy in the Flesh
(New York, Basic Books, 1999, 3)

[36] If you are an atheist, at this point at this point you might
simply say that it is useless to imagine something that
doesn't exist. My suggestion, however, is that you continue
the journey and "try on" the imaginative ideas in this chapter.
Some of them may fit with your beliefs and thus may expand
your horizons of knowing.

[37] This is called the apophatic tradition or approach to
God by theologians. Wikipedia summarises this as
"all descriptions (of God) if attempted will be ultimately
false and conceptualization should be avoided.

[38] New International Version of the Bible, Psalm 8:4

[39] This is the key difference between seeing man as a purely
natural being, evolving like every other animal and seeing man
as having being given something extra at some point, even if
he evolved, that makes him transcendent. Several terms,
which I won't expand on, used for this something extra are
the person's "soul" and God's "grace."

[40] Frederick Neitzsche, Thus Spoke Zarathustra,
Zarathustra's Prologue, http://faculty.washington.edu/cbehler/
teaching/coursenotes/Texts/Zarsel.html

[41] Frederick Neitzsche, Will to Power, quoted in Hegel,
History and Interpretation, edited by Shaun Gallegher, SUNY
Series in Hegelian Studies (Albany, NY, SUNY Press, 1997), 92.

[42] Clare Mann's website, Existentialism for Everyone,
http://lifemyths.com/existentialtherapy/existential-
psychotherapy-values-assumptions-underpinning-practice/

[43] Jean-Paul Sartre, http://www.goodreads.com/author/
quotes/1466.Jean_Paul_Sartre?auto_login_attempted = true

[44] From the Upanishads,
http://en.wikipedia.org/wiki/Kena_Upanishad

[45] Of course, one can imagine a cosmic battle between good gods and evil gods, and many human cultures have done this. I am imagining one God, not many, and a "good" God rather than a sinister one.

[46] We can also choose not to choose, to say with one friend of mine, "My philosophy of life is not to have a philosophy. Life just is; s__t happens. If there is a purpose to life, so what? It's not important to me."

[47] Rahner, Ibid, p 116

[48] Julian of Norwich,
 http://en.wikipedia.org/wiki/Julian_of_Norwich

[49] Victor Frankl, Man's Search for Meaning, quote from Wikipedia, http://en.wikipedia.org/wiki/ Man's_Search_for_Meaning

[50] Viktor Frankl at Ninety, an interview by Matthew Scully, First Things, April 1995, http://www.firstthings.com/ article/2008/08/004-viktor-frankl-at-ninety-an-interview-18

[51] Daniel Dennett, Darwin's Dangerous Idea; Evolution and the Meanings of Life (New York, NY, Simon & Schuster, 1995), p370 - 371

[52] I suggest you read Tarnas's book, The Passion of the Western Mind and Gilson's Metodical Realism to understand this assertion.

[53] Richard Tarnas, The Passion of the Western Mind (New York, NY, Ballantine Books, 1991), 402

[54] For a good explanation of the "Brain-centric" and the "Reality-centric" stances, read Methodical Realism by Etienne Gilson. He calls the Brain-centric the Idealist Stance, and the Reality-centric the Realist stance. I have changed these terms to make the stances a bit clearer to non-philosophers.

[55] Each person perceives the world through their own unique "lens," combining both the physical way the brain works with the learning which they have done. The question of truth, however, is different than how the brain works. In the Reality-centric stance, truth is "what is", existing regardless of what a person perceives. We must engage in a quest for truth to determine whether our individual perceptions match this truth.

In the both the Reality-centric and Brain-centric stances, scientists use the scientific method – repeatable experiments and identical results – in a quest for truth to determine the "fit" of scientific theory with reality. For other questions, for which there is no data and no way for the scientific method to be applied, the Brain-centric stance cannot make a statement about truth, while the Reality-centric stance simply states that other methods must be used in the quest for truth.

[56] Counterfeit or mock insights may surface. For example, James Redfield in The Celestine Prophecy says, with other Gnostic "gurus," that reality is hidden and secret, that ordinary people need special wisdom to see it. This denies that man has built-in capacity to know reality which is the fundamental assumption of the "Reality-centric" stance. Our intellects are made to know reality, and its secrets are there to be freely discovered by anyone, in day to day life.

[57] The Brain-centric stance assumes that thinking is only an organic process, based on a series of operations of a computer-like brain. The Reality-centric stance sees the human intellect as a higher order transcendent capability, not reducible to strictly computer-like knowing.

[58] Rollo May, The Cry for Myth
(New York, NY, W.W. Norton, 1991)

[59] Charles Handy, The Hungry Spirit
(New York, NY, Broadway Books, 1998)

[60] Emily Dickinson, 'T IS so much joy!,
http://www.bartleby.com/113/1004.html

[61] New International Version of the Bible, Psalm 46:10

[62] George Meredith,
http://www.poetryfoundation.org/poem/173964#

[63] Ranier Maria Rilke,
http://www.poemhunter.com/poem/buddha-in-glory/

[64] St John of the Cross, http://en.wikipedia.org/wiki/
Ascent_of_Mount_Carmel#Text_of_the_Poem

[65] New International Version of the Bible, Proverbs,
excerpts from Chapter 8

[66] Rainer Maria Rilke,
http://www.poemhunter.com/poem/you-you-only-exist/

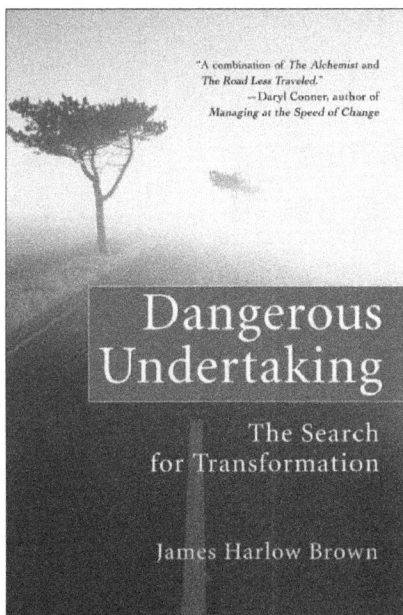

"A combination of *The Alchemist* and *The Road Less Traveled.*"
—Daryl Conner, author of
Managing at the Speed of Change

Dangerous Undertaking

The Search for Transformation

James Harlow Brown

If you enjoyed *Imagining Rama*,
read *Dangerous Undertaking;*
The Search for Transformation
by James Harlow Brown.
The Introduction and Chapter 1 follow.

Dangerous Undertaking

The Search for Transformation

By James Harlow Brown

Introduction

We have lost our magic in today's world yet it still exists. *Dangerous Undertaking* is a story about a man who encountered that magic, in the form of a chance meeting on a plane with a strange and wise man. He became a different man, making revolutionary changes yet, in the beginning, he did not believe in magic. Could this happen to you? Read and decide for yourself.

Why is it so important to find this magic? In a word, the world is in crisis. Crisis means threat, risk, danger. Yet seen through a different lens a crisis is an opportunity for a fresh beginning, the advent of a new way of thinking, the potential for a return to health. There are many voices telling us about the risks of the crisis we face today. Some are even saying that the human race has gone too far and now even our planet is at risk. But there are other voices—muted and thoughtful, yet powerful and connected to the magic—describing our current crisis as a wonder-filled time when something new is emerging. Thomas Berry, Paul Hawken, Nicholas Kittrie, Walter Brueggemann to name a few. *Dangerous Undertaking* presents their hopeful insights so that many people will experience the thrill of searching for the magic and understanding their own creative role in resolving the current crisis.

Why is the magic essential? Why can't we solve the issues by ourselves? We don't know how and we don't have enough power. A problem has gradually emerged during the last hundred years that we all experience but don't yet comprehend. More and more, our lives are controlled by large organizations that lack sensitivity to issues that are vital to us. This is problematic, both on a personal and a global level. Many people feel under-utilized and even exploited in their work. Their 'real' self and dreams aren't appreciated by the power structure that constrains them. Organizations, in general, are largely ignoring the crisis our planet faces in the 21st century.

Most of us cope with these problems by cutting them down to size and dealing with their effects in our family, our job, our community. This is a good beginning but we must not cede the management of the world to the leaders in power. We must not ignore changing "the system," the economic, political, religious and social forces that keeps the world on the risky track it is currently on. Our individual magic is essential. I believe strongly that the moral 'DNA' of large institutions and society at large first emerges in the hearts of committed individuals who care deeply about the future.

There is nothing new about this challenge. The human spirit has been transforming the world for thousands of years. We all know stories about individual change agents like Jesus, the Buddha, Martin Luther King and Nelson Mandela. Perhaps in the 21st century we should simply be patient and depend on the emergence of such extraordinary people to "save our bacon." I believe we are called to do our part, not simply wait and pray. The 'little people'—the Frodos and Parsifals—must find the magic and act because of the urgency of the situation.

At the end of the book, there is a set of discussion questions and a Bibliography for further exploration of the concepts presented. My hope is that forward-thinking leaders in large organizations will sponsor discussion groups, as a courageous first step toward the moral transformation of large organizations that is so badly needed.

Chapter 1

Life is a quest, not a contest. Frank O'Connor showed me that. When I first met him on a night flight to Australia I was driving my life in the fast lane. 'Perform, Achieve, Succeed' was my roadmap. I didn't let anything get in my way and didn't slow down to solve problems like 'world hunger' or how people felt. The world is a tough place. Life is a competition that doesn't have a happy ending unless you win. That was how I thought before I met Frank.

So what? you ask. Aren't there millions of people like me, trying to make it big in the world? You're right of course, but I was lucky enough to meet Frank. He transformed me when I had absolutely no reason to change. Think of me as being imprisoned in something like a cave—not a completely dark one, actually a well furnished one, but a cave nonetheless. Some time in my past I had unknowingly confined myself there. As a result I could only see and move in very limited ways. If I had looked in the right direction I might have seen a light that signaled there was an exit. It never occurred to me. My tight little universe met all my needs—and no one else's. Even now it's hard for me to explain exactly how I escaped. The best I can do is tell my story and let you decide.

By the way, I'm Neil Armstrong Schmidt. Yeah, I know, like the astronaut. I was born on July 22, 1969, two days after the first moon walk. My father, in a fit of patriotism or wanting me to be great or something, named me after him. As you'll soon see, I'm not a hero like the astronaut, but I have been fortunate to meet a few that I will tell you about.

I went to Australia several times a year to 'juice up' our distributors and get them to push our products harder. On this particular trip, as always, I had flown from Washington DC to Los Angeles, coped with the usual two hour wait in the QANTAS Lounge and finally boarded the 747. It was after midnight Washington time and all I wanted was to stretch out in Business Class and get to sleep as fast as possible. LA to Sydney takes about fourteen hours and I had a routine. Tell the flight attendant I didn't want to eat or be woken up, wear the blindfold and earplugs from the courtesy pack and—most importantly—*not* start a conversation with my seat mate. But that night I was restless and for some reason couldn't sleep.

The upper deck cabin was dark when I finally gave up and decided to find a magazine. The man next to me in the aisle seat had his light on and was reading a book that must have been very interesting because he was busily underlining and making notes in the margin. I needed to get past, but didn't want to break his concentration so I sat, outside his little cone of light, waiting for the right moment.

He looked to be about sixty and was kind of weather-beaten with short-cropped gray hair. He seemed quite tall and was slouched down in his seat with his legs stretched out under the seat in front of him. He had on Levis and a black sweater (called a 'jumper' in Australia where we were headed).

Suddenly, he closed his book, folded up his tray table and stood up. Great! Now I could easily get out without the squirming, twisting contortions it usually took.

While I was unbuckling my seat belt I glanced at the cover of the book he'd left lying on his seat. *The Homeless Mind*. Never heard of it. I got up and walked toward the rear of the cabin. He was standing there, waiting for a toilet. He was tall. Probably six four. Even taller than me. I nodded to him and walked back to the galley to get a bottle of water from the flight attendant. I did some stretches for a few minutes to get the kinks out and returned to my seat. He got up to let me past and vaguely smiled at me then continued to read and underline his book.

After a few minutes he turned to me and said, "Hi, I'm Frank O'Connor," giving me what I came to recognize as his 'Gandalf' look.' I like to use the wizard from *The Lord of the Rings* to describe Frank because that's how he affected me from the very beginning. Maybe he thought I was a little like Frodo too.

He stuck out his hand. It was large and rough, his handshake firm, like the farmer's son I learned he was. He was a management consultant, an American who made his home in London. I told him what I did and we chatted a bit. Then I asked him about the book he was reading. Why did I do that? It wasn't like me— Mr. Perform, Achieve, Succeed—to waste my time on conversation with a total stranger. Like I said, I can't explain why Frank was able to reach me inside my cave.

"I'm curious about the book you're reading. *The Homeless Mind*. How could your mind be homeless? It's part of you. Puzzling idea."

He gave me a searching look, maybe measuring my question against some criteria he had. Was it worth spending time answering? I must have passed because he immediately took our conversation to another level.

"Let me tell you what it's about, but not how you probably expect me to. It may take some time. Are you interested?"

He paused and waited for me to choose. I didn't actually care that much about *The Homeless Mind,* but I was intrigued by his response.

He must have seen the yes on my face because he quickly asked, "What are you thinking about, Neil?"

"That either you might be nuts or that this might turn out to be a really interesting flight."

He grinned at me and returned my volley.

"I suppose, in a way, I am nuts as you say. Like the authors of *The Homeless Mind,* I look at the world from a different perspective. Have you ever seen those odd 3-D pictures in newspapers or magazines? They look all garbled; you can't see anything but strange colored lines and shapes mixed together. Nothing coherent. But if you look at them in a certain way you'll see surprising images emerge from the jumbled picture. That's what I do: look at our human situation in a slightly out of focus way and find patterns that most people overlook."

"So, what have you found? Net it out for me."

That was Neil the Executive speaking. Impatient. Don't beat around the bush. Give me a sound bite if you want to hold my attention.

"I can't. If I tried to explain the patterns it would be like me telling you there are three dolphins hidden in one of those 3-D pictures. You need to see the dolphins for yourself. It's very difficult for you to see the patterns because if you're like most people your mind is stuck in a rut. You see the world in very limited ways. I help people find ways to get out of their rut and see these important patterns."

It was obvious he was encouraging me to give it a go. He started working on my 'mind in a rut' problem immediately.

"Remember the old saying that we can't see the forest for the trees? Try this little experiment. Imagine seeing the earth from outer space, say from the moon. Can you picture it? You can't see very much detail at all. The earth looks like a blue, brown, and white ball. Even when you're only a few hundred miles away you can't see anything man-made, not even large cities or the Great Wall of China. Now imagine you are on the surface, in some city. All you can see is detail. There is so much detail that you're in information-overload. You simply can't see the world the same way you can from space. What I'm trying to say is that too much information is what blinds you to the hidden patterns I see and keeps you in a rut. You need to leave all this information behind, get some altitude above your ordinary life so to speak to be able to see them. You follow me so far?"

Yeah. We can't see Frank's patterns and details at the same time. What we see depends on our perspective. I still didn't get what he meant by patterns, but at that moment I was more interested in watching Frank's face than in what he was saying. His expression fascinated me. It combined intense concentration with a kind of peacefulness, like he was aware of something that I wasn't.

"So, here's a question for you, Neil. How do we escape from all that information?"

He waited for my answer. He reminded me of a teacher trying to make me use my mind more than I usually did.

Just then the 747 started to shake, and then it gave us a really good bounce. We must have been getting near the equator where the captain had told us the winds would be a bit rough. The plane's computer smoothed out the flight as best it could, but the pilot kept the 'fasten seat belt' light on.

"That was interesting," Frank said. "Did you feel the autopilot kick in and get control of the plane?"

I had a thought.

"Frank, what if our mind is in a rut because it's on some kind of autopilot too? What if, to get rid of all the information and see things from a fresh perspective, we have to turn off this autopilot and, in a way, take control over flying our own mind?"

He looked at me with a big grin.

"That's a darn good way to put it. I like your autopilot metaphor. But the problem is still there. Where is the switch to our autopilot? How do we turn it off?"

He waited a moment, but, when I had a blank look, answered his own question.

"Maybe something happens to us. Something completely unexpected grabs our attention and wrenches us out of our rut. It may be something simple, not out of the ordinary at all. There is a story about how something like this happened to the poet Dante. He once met a young woman on the streets of Florence who simply smiled at him and said good morning as she passed. He spent more than half of his life wrestling with the impact of that meeting. The young girl became Dante's heavenly escort Beatrice in his great poem *The Divine Comedy*. He was yanked out of his rut by that encounter. What happened? Maybe it was like a door opening, very briefly, and he caught a glimpse of something through the crack, something that fascinated him and wouldn't let his mind rest until he figured it out. Who knows?"

I imagined Dante meeting the young girl and having a stunned expression on his face. How did that fit me? I wasn't a poet. Poets are always seeing things that the rest of us don't. It felt like Frank was playing a game with me. That seemed kind of bizarre. I wasn't sure I wanted to play, but I decided to go along with him for a while.